JEWISH SPORTS STARS

ATHLETIC
HEROES
PAST AND
PRESENT

DAVID J. GOLDMAN

KAR-BEN
PUBLISHING

To my sister, Sharon Goldman Lerner, and cousin, Jay David Kremen, who were stars to me and loved sports in their own way, and to Jeremy Glick and the other athlete-heroes of Flight 93. —D.J.G.

KAR-BEN PUBLISHING, INC.
A division of Lerner Publishing Group
241 First Avenue North
Minneapolis, MN 55401 U.S.A.
800-4KARBEN

Website address: www.karben.com

Library of Congress Cataloging-in-Publication Data

Goldman, David J.
    Jewish sports stars : athletic heroes past and present / by David J. Goldman.
       p.   cm.
    Summary: Describes the lives and achievements of prominent Jewish-American sports heroes, such as Sandy Koufax, Kerri Strug, and Mark Spitz.
    Includes bibliographical references and index.
    ISBN: 1–58013–085–2 (pbk. : alk. paper)
    1. Jewish athletes—United States—Biography—Juvenile literature. [1. Jewish athletes. 2. Athletes.] I. Title.
    GV697.G524 2004
    796'.089'924073—dc22   2003015801

Manufactured in the United States of America
1 2 3 4 5 6 – JR – 09 08 07 06 05 04

TABLE OF CONTENTS

Mike Rossman, *right,* **throws a punch at Victor Galindez during a bout in 1978. Rossman won by knockout in thirteen rounds.**

FOREWORD

Growing up, I would sometimes visit the Men's Health Club at our local JCC. There was a pool table, a ping-pong table, and the prerequisite steam bath and whirlpool. I was too young to enter on my own, but my father would take me there once a month. While I wouldn't admit it then, I did actually enjoy listening to the old guys talking sports. On occasion I would hear, with proud voices, talk of Jewish boxers who would wear the Star of David on their trunks. I had only vaguely heard these names before, and sometimes in a different context—the name Benny Leonard, for instance, was much more familiar to me as an AZA youth group chapter. I knew it was unlikely that I'd actually see a Jewish boxer on television.

From time to time, I would turn on the fights, and one night I found myself watching a light heavyweight bout between the formidable champion Victor Galindez and a smaller fighter sporting a mop of dark, curly hair named Mike Rossman. I noticed Rossman had an icon of some kind on his trunks, but it was small and the picture was a little grainy. Could this be a modern version of one of the revered Jewish boxers the old men at the health club reminisced about? Even though the announcers barely gave Rossman a chance, he was fighting gamely and I started to pay more attention. After studying the screen closely from various angles, I realized Rossman was indeed wearing a Star of David. Instinctively, I felt a great sense of pride, and, though I often cheered for the underdog during boxing matches, I felt this was an extremely special moment. Rossman did go on to upset Galindez, and there hasn't been a Jewish boxing champion since. This was the start of my search for modern Jewish athletes.

We live in a sports-crazy world, and I count myself as one of the crazed. For a few, sports are big business, and for fewer still, they are a profession. As fans, we tend to identify with the players on our home teams. We have a more personal experience when we are able to connect as a fan to athletes who may identify with us as well. Jews are a very small minority in the United States, and nowhere is this more obvious than in our national sports scene. Growing up, I wanted to become a professional athlete because to me this represented the accumulation of hard work, talent, popularity, and luck. When I noticed that an athlete was Jewish, I found that I was able to identify more personally with his/her success and failure. We all have our own personal stories of Jewish pride, but my first was Rossman defeating Galindez. I hope this book will inspire a few more.

—Adam Lerner
Publisher, Kar-Ben Publishing

BASEBALL

Hank Greenberg in his Tigers uniform

HANK GREENBERG

Born: January 1, 1911, New York, NY
Died: September 4, 1986

We shall miss him in the infield and shall miss him at the bat. But he's true to his religion—and I honor him for that!

—Edgar Guest, from his poem about Hank Greenberg's observance of Yom Kippur

When baseball fans talk about the best home run hitters of old, the same names always seem to pop up—"The Great Bambino" Babe Ruth, Mickey Mantle, "Joltin' Joe" DiMaggio, Roger Maris, Willie Mays, and Hank Aaron. Seldom mentioned is the Jewish sports hero "Hammerin' Hank" Greenberg, who smashed 58 home runs in 1938 and hit 331 total home runs in a career cut short by military service. Greenberg's accomplishments have often been overshadowed by the celebrity players of his day such as Babe Ruth. But Hank's career was a memorable one that paved the way for many Jewish athletes to come.

Henry Benjamin Greenberg, nicknamed Hank, was born in the Bronx, New York, on January 1, 1911. His parents were Orthodox Jews from Romania and brought up Hank in a small and simple home. Hank's parents must have known that their son was going to lead a life very different from theirs when they watched him grow to a muscular six feet four inches tall. They were always supportive of Hank's unique athletic talent, watching from the stands as he excelled in nearly every sport he played.

Hank attended James Monroe High School in the Bronx, where he lettered in four sports, but baseball was always Hank's first love. "Baseball," Hank once said, "was the only sport that really mattered . . . the only game you could find on the sports pages." Even as a gawky youth, Hank could smack towering home runs that left his opponents breathless. And what he lacked in the game's fundamentals, he made up for with hard work and grueling practice.

After high school, Hank played for local teams and thought about college at New York University (NYU). It came as a bit of a surprise when major-league scouts appeared at his games and started offering him large cash bonuses. One afternoon, the famous Yankee scout Paul Krichell watched as Hank hit three home runs in an amateur league game. After the game, he offered Hank a thousand dollars on the spot to sign with the Yankees. A few weeks later, a scout from the Washington Senators promised Hank a ten thousand dollar bonus. But it was the Detroit Tigers who finally won the bid for Greenberg. They offered him nine thousand dollars (three thousand of it immediately) and would wait for him to go to college. Hank signed with the Tigers.

Education was very important to Hank, but after one semester at NYU, he was burning to play ball again. Spring training rolled around, and Hank could not keep away from the game. He called the Tigers and asked to join the club immediately. They were more than happy to take him early. And after proving himself in the minor leagues, Hank Greenberg was called up to the majors in 1933.

Hank didn't play full-time his first year. He played first base and had to trade off with the other first baseman, Harry Davis. But when he got his at bats, he made the most of them, batting .301 for the season and showing his potential for long-ball hitting with 12 home runs. He also batted in an impressive 87 runs. The Tigers could no longer ignore this rookie slugger.

The year 1934 was Hank's breakout season. He secured the job as the Tigers' first baseman and earned his keep by batting .339 and leading the league in doubles with 63. He smashed 26 home runs and had 139 runs batted in (RBIs). The Tigers made it to the World Series that year, and although they didn't capture the title, Hank batted a solid .321 and knocked in 7 RBIs.

Hank's career on the field was going brilliantly, and he seemed to be a star of limitless potential. But off the field, Hank faced the hardships of being the first huge Jewish sports star. "After all," said Hank, "I was representing a couple of million Jews among a hundred million gentiles and I was always in the spotlight." Though the Jewish community adored him, Hank experienced harsh anti-Semitism from fans and opponents. He was attacked both physically and through the use of slurs. Hank commented once in an interview, "It was a constant thing . . . . Not only were you a bum, you were a Jewish bum."

Despite a sometimes hostile environment, Hank Greenberg was not to be discouraged. He was a rising star, and in 1935 he proved it by earning the American League Most Valuable Player (MVP) award, a shoe-in for the prize. He led the league with 36 homers and 170 RBIs. And for the third year in a row, he batted safely over .300 with an average of .328. The Tigers made it to the World Series again that year and won, defeating the Chicago Cubs in six games. Unfortunately, Hank could only play in the first two games of the series due to a fractured wrist.

Hank hit his peak in 1938. It was a magical season from start to finish. He hit 58 home runs (just two shy of Ruth's record at the time) and knocked in 146 runs. He batted over .300 again, had 11 two-home run games, and hit 12 home runs in his last 24 games. Sportswriters soon placed his name with the best sluggers of the time along with Babe Ruth and Jimmy Foxx.

Hank played another couple of great seasons, winning another MVP in 1940, before he shocked the sports world by enlisting to fight in World War II. The young man who served his religion by often refusing to play ball on the High Holidays wanted to serve his country and help defeat Nazism. He could have avoided combat if he'd wanted to, but it was important for Hank to do his part. Most people saw his actions as nothing short of heroic, but fans sorely missed his home run swing during the war.

When he returned from combat, Hank continued to play well, but he didn't have the speed and athleticism that he had possessed in the late 1930s. He retired in 1947, after playing a season in the National League with the Pittsburgh Pirates. In 1956 he was inducted into the Hall of Fame. He passed away thirty years later, after a successful second career as a businessman and sports executive.

It remains a mystery how many records Hank Greenberg would have broken if he had not left the game in his prime to serve his country. But he accomplished spectacular feats in the face of adversity and was a hero to those who fought discrimination and hatred everywhere. Later, baseball great Al Rosen called Hank a "pathfinder" for Jewish ballplayers. He was a profound athlete but also a modest and dutiful man, and his name deserves to live among the legends of the game.

SANDY KOUFAX

Born: December 30, 1935,
Brooklyn, NY

*I expect him to pitch a
no-hit, no-run game every
time he starts. I'm only
surprised when somebody
gets a hit off him.*

> —*teammate Don Drysdale
> on Sandy Koufax*

**Sandy Koufax struck out 18 Chicago Cubs
(setting a National League daytime record)
during this game in 1962.**

It is difficult to choose one pitcher to call the greatest in the history of baseball. There have been many inspiring candidates over the years, and the list is growing. But a case can certainly be made for the Jewish left-hander, Sandy Koufax. With his four no-hitters and league-leading earned run average (ERA) from 1962 to 1966, Koufax dominated the Major Leagues in the 1960s and entered the Hall of Fame in 1972 with record-breaking numbers.

Born Sanford Koufax on December 30, 1935, the future fast-baller grew up in a Brooklyn home with no baseball fans. Sandy's father was a lawyer and paid little attention to professional sports. And when Sandy first discovered his athletic talent, it was on the basketball court instead of the baseball diamond. During his childhood, Sandy could often be found at the Jewish Community House in Brooklyn practicing jump shots or playing a pickup game. He didn't think of trying out for his school baseball team until he was a senior at Lafayette High School.

Sandy played first base on the high school team and only pitched when he was on the sandlot with his friends. But he soon became famous around the neighborhood for his fastball. The owner of the neighborhood's sporting goods store tipped off a local sportswriter about Sandy's speed. Soon there were scouts from the Brooklyn Dodgers watching him pitch. By the time he was a sophomore in college, Sandy Koufax had received an offer from the Dodgers.

He got off to a shaky start in the majors, struggling with his speed and control. He struck out 18 Giants in one game in 1959, but after that, his pitching was erratic and unpredictable. It wasn't until 1961 that Sandy began to develop into the pitcher whom fans would remember.

Sandy's fellow Jewish teammate, Norm Sherry, gave him some valuable advice. Sitting with Sandy on the team bus one day, Norm said, "Sandy, I think your troubles would be solved if you would just try to throw easier, throw more changeups, just get the ball over." Norm's simple advice paid off.

In 1961 Sandy won 18 games and broke the National League record for the most strikeouts. In 1962, despite an injury, he pitched a no-hitter, was selected for the All-Star Game, and became the first major league pitcher to have two games in which he struck out 18 batters. In 1963 Sandy won 25 games and pitched his second no-hitter. *Time* magazine named him the best pitcher of the year.

Sandy also made headlines in 1963 for organizing his pitching around the Jewish High Holidays. He pitched on only two days' rest at times in order to have the holidays off, earning him the respect of the Jewish community. The Dodgers won the National League pennant that year, and Sandy ended the season with an earned run average of 1.88, the prestigious Cy Young award, and the league's MVP award. In the postseason, he won two games in the World Series, helping his team capture the world championship against the New York Yankees.

Although 1963 was great for Sandy, late in the season in 1964 he started complaining about his elbow. He was forced to cut the season short after winning 19 games. He had pitched a great season, with three no-hitters, but his injury left him uncertain of the future.

In 1965 Sandy was diagnosed with "traumatic arthritis," but even with his ailing arm, Sandy managed to dominate, winning 26 games and pitching a perfect game (a no-hitter with no walks) against the Chicago Cubs. He became the first Major League pitcher to throw four no-hitters. The Dodgers returned to the World Series that season, and Sandy found his name in the news for actions both on and off the field.

The first game of the 1965 World Series against the Minnesota Twins fell on Yom Kippur, the holiest day of the year for Jews, and Sandy told his coach that he would not pitch. The Dodgers were crushed to find out that he would not start the series as planned. Sandy stayed firm in his belief that the holiday was more important than any game, even a World Series. Despite his absence in the first contest, the Dodgers went on to win the series in seven games, and Sandy received his second Cy Young award.

The year 1966 was Sandy's last year in the majors. His arthritis forced him into early retirement, but not before one last memorable season. Although he didn't control every at bat like he used to, Sandy won 27 games in 1966 and struck out over 300 batters. In 1972 he became the youngest player ever to be inducted into the Hall of Fame. At 36 years old, Sandy received the highest total number of Hall of Fame votes. In a short major league career, Sandy Koufax had won the admiration of the entire baseball world and had earned himself a place among baseball's greatest.

SHAWN GREEN

Born: November 10, 1972, Des Plaines, IL

Being Jewish is something different, and I understand that, it'll be something that differentiates me from other players—always separates me.

—*Shawn Green*

Shawn Green blasts his fourth home run of the day versus the Milwaukee Brewers, May 23, 2002.

Shawn Green is the embodiment of the modern baseball star. As opposed to many of the all-time greats, who specialized in a particular skill, Shawn can do it all. He can hit for power, hit for average, field, throw, even steal bases. And with his selfless devotion to the Jewish community, Shawn might just be the new model for Jewish athletes.

Born in Des Plaines, Illinois, on November 10, 1972, Shawn David Green also lived in New Jersey before his family settled in California. His father, Ira, played college basketball for DePaul University and was a huge baseball fan. Shawn's family could not have been happier when he became an undeniable baseball talent in high school. A first-team selection in the 1991 *USA Today* All-USA high school team and a 4.0 student, Shawn garnered praise for his skills on and off the diamond at an early age.

Shawn earned a baseball scholarship to Stanford and then, in 1991, was selected by the Toronto Blue Jays as the sixteenth overall pick in the free-agent draft. Shawn enrolled in Stanford in the fall, planning to go to school before hitting the pros, but like Hank Greenberg, he had a passion to play baseball full time. He joined the Blue Jays and was a September call-up in 1993. Thus he started his major-league career with a World Series ring. Although Shawn did not play in the series, the ring was an appropriate start to a career that would soon be full of awards and accolades.

In 1994 Shawn played most of the season for Syracuse in the International League to hone his skills. After winning the league's Rookie of the Year award and the MVP award, he was placed in the Blue Jays lineup for the 1995 season. He had a solid year, batting just under .300 with 15 home runs and 54 RBIs.

Shawn came into his own during the 1998 season. His average was a stable .278, but his other statistics exploded. Shawn hit 35 home runs, batted in 100 runs, and stole 35 bases. He became only the ninth player in the history of the American League to hit 30 home runs and steal 30 bases in a season. Shawn attributed his success to the hard work he had put in trying to carve himself a spot in the majors. "You don't learn much by having things come easy," he said.

In the seasons that followed, Shawn continued to work hard and his numbers continued to rise. In 1999 Shawn batted .309

and hit 42 homers. He knocked in 123 runs and had a slugging percentage of .588. He also nabbed a Gold Glove award for his excellent work in the outfield and played in the All-Star Game. Shawn was fast approaching the ranks of superstardom. And he never forgot the support of his Jewish community.

Shawn has taken advantage of his status as a high-profile athlete to lend his voice and his name to Jewish organizations. He has participated in the Jewish Big Brother program and has become the spokesman for KOREH, a Jewish coalition for literacy. When he was traded to the Dodgers for the 2000 season, Shawn made the most of living in Los Angeles, where the community welcomed him with open arms. Before he arrived, a seventy-five-foot mural of Shawn was painted on Dodger Stadium.

By the 2001 season, Shawn was one of the best hitters in the game. He slammed 49 home runs and had 125 RBIs, while also boasting career highs in slugging percentage and total bases. After going to the All-Star Game for the third consecutive season, Shawn hit 29 of his 49 home runs.

The 2002 season proved no different. Shawn blasted 42 home runs and had 114 RBIs. On May 23, 2002, Shawn went six for six, with four home runs in one game. It was the single greatest individual hitting day in the history of major-league baseball. In the next two games, Shawn hit three home runs, giving him seven in three games. This was another all-time record.

Shawn Green has risen to an elite status that most athletes only dream of. People have called him the Hank Greenberg of modern times, a compliment that Shawn relishes. With more seasons ahead, Shawn could retire as one of the best that has ever played the game. He is a model Jewish athlete and a point of pride for all his supporters.

MORE JEWISH MAJOR LEAGUERS:

Al "Flip" Rosen, the Cleveland Indians' third baseman, won the American League MVP award in 1953. He batted .336 that season, with 43 home runs and 145 RBIs. Rosen was a four-time All-Star and drove in 100 runs for five seasons straight. He followed Hank Greenberg's path by refusing to play on the High Holidays. When he was inducted into the Jewish Sports Hall of Fame he remarked, "At no time have I been so deeply moved as I have been this evening to be recognized a Jew by Jews." He was a baseball executive for many years.

In the late 1960s and early 1970s, **Ken Holtzman**, a Jewish southpaw, threw two no-hitters for the Chicago Cubs. He joined the Oakland A's in 1972 and won at least 18 games for the next four seasons. In 1973 Ken went 21–13 with a 2.97 ERA. He led the A's to three World Championship titles from 1972–1974, with a total World Series record of 4–1. Ken was also famous off the field for trying to keep the kosher dietary laws while traveling with the team.

Steve Stone was a hit-and-miss Jewish pitcher in the 1970s, but in 1980, he had a nearly perfect season for the Baltimore Orioles. Steve won 25 games that season, 14 of them in a row. He retired nine straight batters in the All-Star Game and finished the year with a Cy Young award. After Steve retired from the game in 1982, he became an announcer for the Chicago Cubs.

Gabe Kapler has proved to be a promising Jewish outfielder with the Texas Rangers, the Colorado Rockies, and the Boston Red Sox. In the 2000 season, Gabe set a Rangers record with a 28-game hitting streak and batted a sound .302. In 2002 he was called, "the most athletic and most versatile" of the Texas outfielders by manager Jerry Narron. He moved to the Rockies midseason that year, where he hit .311 with three triples. In 2003 he signed with the Boston Red Sox and had a solid year.

Catcher **Brad Ausmus** has been a reliable and talented player with both the Detroit Tigers and the Houston Astros. He is considered one of the best defensive catchers in the game and was rewarded for his skills by making the All-Star team in 1999. Brad is a good offensive player, batting just under .300 in 1995 and .275 in 1997. He also has good speed and a lethal arm for throwing out opposing base stealers.

Another gifted Jewish catcher is **Mike Lieberthal** of the Philadelphia Phillies. Mike is a power-hitting Gold Glover who made the All-Star team in both 1999 and 2000. In 1999 he slammed 31 homers and had 96 RBIs. He smacked 29 doubles in the 2002 season and hit 15 home runs, in addition to catching almost every game.

Mike Lieberthal, *left,* **forces the Cardinal's Ray Lankford out at home, then throws to first to complete a double play, August 11, 1999.**

BASKETBALL

DOLPH SCHAYES

Born: May 19, 1928,
New York, NY

He was in the gym practicing every spare minute. We had to chase him out.

—*NYU coach Howard Cann on Dolph Schayes*

Before basketball was a national phenomenon and fast-paced televised games attracted millions of viewers, players were working each night to hone their skills. Jewish superstar Dolph Schayes was one such pioneer. His powerful driving style and smooth shot helped pave the way for dynamic players such as Michael Jordan and Kobe Bryant. Many sports historians consider Schayes to be one of the best to ever grace the court.

Dolph Schayes, *left,* **is often considered the first modern basketball player.**

Adolph Schayes, better known as Dolph, was born May 19, 1928, into a family obsessed with sports. Dolph's father, who almost became a professional fighter in his youth, often took Dolph and his two brothers to sports events at Madison Square Garden in New York City. His father was proud and supportive when Dolph made the basketball team at DeWitt Clinton High School in the Bronx.

Like many young players of great height, the six-foot-eight-inch Dolph was clumsy at first and had problems controlling his lanky frame. But Dolph was a hard worker, and as his future NYU coach would say, "His mind was set on being great." In high school and later at college, Dolph was often the first one on the court at practice and the last one to leave. He improved greatly by his senior year at NYU, graduating with 815 total points in 80 games. Dolph soon received offers from professional teams.

Both the New York Knicks and the Syracuse Nationals wanted Dolph to play in the pros, and he surprised many by choosing Syracuse. He later told interviewers that he wanted to start off with smaller crowds, before he began to play in high-profile games. Dolph enjoyed what he called, "the camaraderie of the small town fans," and his exciting play soon made him a favorite with the locals. He was named Rookie of the Year in the National Basketball League in 1949, averaging 12.8 points a game.

The next year, the Syracuse Nationals moved to the National Basketball Association (NBA), and Dolph led the team in scoring with 16.8 points a game. The Nationals went all the way to the finals that season with a record of 51–13. Although the team fell in the finals to the Minneapolis Lakers, it was a standout season for Dolph, as he became a star.

In the 1954–1955 season, the Nationals captured the NBA championship. They had made the finals three seasons in a row and had won the contest with a close 92–91 victory in game seven of the series. Dolph hit two clutch free throws near the end of the game to give them a 91–90 lead. He had become a celebrated player, competing and winning in front of huge crowds.

Throughout the 1950s and into the early 1960s, Dolph was one of the premier players in the NBA. He was constantly on the list of league leaders in scoring, shooting, and rebounding, and he made the All-Star team an amazing 12 years in a row. The owner of the Nationals, Danny Biasone, once said of his prize player, "Dolph is the greatest all-around basketball player of all time."

By the time he retired in 1964, Dolph was the NBA's all-time leading scorer with 19,247 career points. At the time, that was 2,800 more points than any player had ever scored. He was also first on the list of career free throws and fourth in career rebounds. In addition, Dolph was one of the most enduring players in the game. From 1951 to 1962, he played in 706 consecutive games. Even after he was the best in the game, he still practiced long and hard. "You can always be a better shot, can't you?" he often said.

After leaving the game as a player, Dolph brought his hard work ethic and dedication to coaching, winning the Coach of the Year award in 1966 for his work with the Philadelphia 76ers. But Dolph was more than just a star player and coach, he was a trailblazer for the sport. In fact, he is considered by some the first modern basketball player. Instead of waiting for things to happen like other players of that time, Dolph created plays, driving to the hoop and drilling long jumpers if he could not work the ball inside. He was inducted into the NBA Hall of Fame in 1972 and was named to the NBA 50th Anniversary All-Time team in 1996. Dolph's son, Danny Schayes, played in the NBA for 18 seasons.

ART HEYMAN

Born: June 24, 1941, Rockville Center, NY

Many thought he was a Protestant from Connecticut, because they had difficulty comprehending a Jew being a great athlete.

—author Meir Z. Ribalow
on Art Heyman

Art Heyman, *right,* **battles Elgin Baylor for the ball, December 25, 1963.**

When Arthur "Art" Bruce Heyman first began playing for Duke University in 1960, he often received encouraging letters from the local chapter of the Ku Klux Klan. Because Duke was a Methodist school, the Klan simply assumed that Heyman was a Christian and instructed him to keep succeeding in the name of Christian White Supremacy. Little did the organization know that Duke's star forward was a Jewish boy from Rockville Center, New York. At the time of his arrival, few Jewish basketball stars had made their mark since the days of Dolph Schayes. Art would change all that by becoming one of the greatest college basketball players in the history of the sport.

Although Art had a sound career in professional basketball, he was a full-fledged superstar in college. Many consider him to be the first great player to come from Duke and one of the best in the school's entire history. While playing for the Blue Devils between 1960 and 1963, Art was a three-time All-American, an Associated Press (AP) National Player of the Year, a National Collegiate Athletic Association (NCAA) Tournament MVP, and a two-time team captain. He holds the university's record for points per game with 25.1 and is in the top 10 in many other categories. His name is listed with modern stars Grant Hill and Shane Battier in the Duke University record books.

Art was a talented player from the start. Basketball came naturally to him, and his six-foot-five-inch, 200-pound stature only made things easier. His game really started to take off in his sophomore year at Duke. In 1961 he scored 25.2 points a game and nabbed 10.9 rebounds per game. Second in the league in scoring, Art was named AP third team All-America and Converse second team All-America. The Blue Devils had a 22–6 record that season and an AP number ten ranking, mostly due to Art's aggressive scoring and tireless rebounding at both ends of the floor.

In 1962 Art again scored more than 25 points a game, and he upped his rebounding average to 11.2 per game. He repeated his All-America honors and led the team to a 20–5 record. As a junior, Art was being recognized as one of the best competitors in all of college athletics, but he was not satisfied. He had yet to carry his team on a successful NCAA Tournament run. This all changed in his senior season at Duke.

Art was widely recognized as the best player in the NCAA in 1963. Like clockwork, he scored just under 25 points a game and grabbed 10.8 rebounds. But this season was different in one important way—the Blue Devils jelled as a team and reached a number two AP ranking. Their near-perfect record of 24–2 made them a favorite going into the NCAA tournament and brought even more attention to Art. For the first time, he was a first team All-America player and the college player of the year in *Sporting News.*

When it came time for the tournament, Art didn't let the pressure get to him. He scored 22 points in Duke's 81–76 win over NYU and scored 16 with 10 rebounds when the Devils rolled over St. Joseph's, 73–59. This win propelled Duke to their first-ever Final Four appearance. In the national semifinal game, Art was unstoppable with 29 points and 12 rebounds, but the Devils could not stop the future championship team, Loyola. The Blue Devils finished third, and Art was named the Tournament MVP and finished his career at Duke with 1,984 points and 865 rebounds.

In 1963 Art became the only Jewish basketball player to go number one overall in the NBA draft. He went on to play in the NBA and the American Basketball Association (ABA) until 1970, averaging 10.3 points per game in the NBA and 15.4 in the ABA. A reliable and tough professional player, Art Heyman will always be remembered by sports fans for his glory days at Duke University. At a time when the idea of a Jewish basketball star was almost inconceivable, Art battled stereotypes and proved himself a contender. His jersey, number 25, was retired after he left the Blue Devils and will live on as an inspiration to Jewish athletes past and present.

JAMILA WIDEMAN

Jamila Wideman, playing for Stanford in 1997, looks for an open pass.

Born: October 16, 1975, Denver, CO

The boys' team could be walking on the floor to practice, my dinner could be ready at home, but I couldn't get her to leave the court.

—High school coach Ron Moyer on Jamila Wideman

Since the emergence of the Women's National Basketball Association (WNBA) in June 1997, women's basketball in America has grown vastly in popularity. Tens of thousands of fans flock to watch some of the country's best female athletes battle it out in exciting professional games. But the league had its struggles at first, fighting for fans in a traditionally male-dominated sport. It was up to the talented female players to prove they were worth watching. One early star of the league and a WNBA pioneer was Jewish guard Jamila Wideman. Jamila was a clutch shooter and a lightning-quick passer for Stanford University in the late 1990s, and after graduation, she helped the WNBA find its fan base.

Named after Muhammad Ali's first daughter, Jamila Ann Wideman was born October 16, 1975, in Denver, Colorado, to a family of intellectuals. Her father, John Edgar, is a renowned African American writer who played college basketball at Penn State, and her mother, Judy, is a lawyer. During her childhood, Jamila often played basketball with her brothers and was the only girl at an all-boys basketball camp when she was 10. The athletic boys treated Jamila like one of the guys and were often impressed by her speed. This experience, along with her father's pointers, helped Jamila to develop her game at a very young age.

When the Widemans moved to Amherst, Massachusetts, a teacher noticed Jamila playing basketball and suggested she try out for the Amherst Regional High School girls' team. Jamila wowed the coaches at the tryout and became Amherst Regional's starting point guard when she was in seventh grade. She was only four feet six inches at the time but could run circles around her opponents. "All you could see," recalled coach Ron Moyer, "was this wisp of a thing, a ponytail and a basketball. Nobody could take the ball from her." In her senior year in high school, Jamila scored an average of 17 points a game with 6 rebounds, 6 assists, and 6 steals. She led her team to a state title that 1992–1993 season, scoring 27 points with 14 steals in the championship game.

After being named to *USA Today's* First Team All-American and being featured on ESPN's *Scholastic Sports America*, Jamila decided to play at Stanford University. She took over the starting point guard position from her very first day and started the first 29 games of the 1994 season. Jamila scored 6.1 points a game and had 2.9 rebounds and 4.5 assists. She was named Pac-10 All-Freshman and was described by her coach as "what makes us go."

In the years that followed, Jamila led Stanford to three straight NCAA Final Four appearances (1995–1997). Although the team could never quite capture the title, Jamila's personal awards in college were almost countless. She was a Pac-10 All-Conference player in 1996. In 1997 Jamila was on the Pac-10 All-Academic Team and was voted the MVP of the NCAA West Regional Tournament. She graduated from Stanford ranked third in the school's history in assists (585) and steals (255).

After graduation in 1997, Jamila turned professional and was the first-round pick of the newly formed WNBA's Los Angeles Sparks. After learning of Jamila's entrance in the league, the WNBA's president, Val Ackerman, said, "In addition to having outstanding basketball skills, Jamila has tremendous appeal as a leader and a role model, and we are thrilled that she will be a part of the WNBA." Jamila surpassed all expectations her first season, ranking eighth in the league in assists and adding flair to WNBA game play with her unique brand of spry and accurate passing. In 1998 Jamila continued to dominate in the assists category, finishing the season with 57. Her assists to turnover ratio was among the best in the league at 1.68.

Jamila was just as impressive off the court as on it. In 1999 she was honored with the *USA Today Weekend's* Most Caring Athlete Award. She received it for starting a foundation called Hoopin' with Jamila, a program that helped inner-city girls learn the game of basketball as well as the craft of poetry. "What the program is really about," says Jamila, "is expression and about having a voice and about empowering yourself."

Jewish fans perhaps remember Jamila best for her decision to play in Israel in the 1999 off-season. Having never explored her mother's Jewish heritage, Jamila decided to play a season for Elitzur Ramla, a team in a suburb of Tel Aviv. Jamila said, "My Jewish background means a lot to me and this is the first chance I've had to think about it." A chairwoman for another team said, "She makes our league better, and her presence gives women's basketball in this country more credibility among the public."

After a season for Cleveland in 1999 and another for Portland in 2000, the injury-prone Jamila Wideman decided to retire from professional basketball to attend NYU Law School. It has always been one of Jamila's dreams to study civil rights and criminal law. Although she will always be remembered as one of the first great professional women's basketball players, Jamila should also be remembered as a true role model. Her devotion to her fans and her heritage separates her from the average athlete. She is the definition of a Jewish sports star.

MORE JEWISH BASKETBALL STARS:

Another pioneer in professional basketball was the early great **Nat Holman.** Although he never reached the celebrity status of Dolph Schayes, Nat helped revolutionize the game as both a player and a coach. As a player, Nat led the original Celtics to a championship in 1921 with his dazzling passing skills and flawless ball control. The Celtics team was one of the first to use the post and pivot style around the basket. As a coach of City College of New York in 1950, he won the NCAA and

Nat Holman poses with a basketball, December 1928.

National Invitation Tournament (NIT) titles, stressing team basketball and movement off the ball. Nat is a member of the Basketball Hall of Fame, the New York City Basketball Hall of Fame, and the International Jewish Sports Hall of Fame. He once told an interviewer, "While I always played at my very best, I tried even harder when I knew the Jewish community was rooting for me."

Following in the footsteps of Art Heyman was another college basketball superstar, **Ernie Grunfeld.** Born in Romania, Ernie moved to New York and became a starter on his high school basketball team. In 1973 he was the only high school player to represent the United States in the Maccabiah Games. He led the team in scoring with 20 points per game and was recruited by colleges the country over. Grunfeld chose Tennessee and became a star point guard, playing alongside another future pro, **Bernard King.** The two were called "The Bernie and Ernie Show," and they appeared on the covers of sports magazines throughout the mid-1970s. Ernie averaged 25.3 points per game his junior year and 23.8 his senior year. Before going pro, he earned a gold medal with the 1976 U.S. Olympic Team. Shortly after the victory, he was chosen by the Milwaukee Bucks in the first round of the NBA draft. He went on to play for the Kansas

City Kings and the New York Knicks, excelling in the NBA until 1986. In 1999 he became the general manager of the Milwaukee Bucks, and in 2003, he became the president of basketball operations for the Washington Wizards.

Larry Brown, one of the best U.S. basketball coaches, is known for turning around downtrodden teams. He played professional basketball for six different ABA teams in six seasons. He has also coached numerous NBA, ABA, and NCAA teams and has been named Coach of the Year several times. Larry coaches the Detroit Pistons and will be leading the U.S. basketball team to the 2004 Olympics. He is the first U.S. male ever to both play and coach in the Olympic Games.

Described as the "Mother of Women's Basketball," Jewish athlete **Senda Berenson** was the first to adapt the game for female competition. A friend of basketball inventor Dr. James Naismith, Senda edited the original rules book for women's basketball in the late 1800s and the early 1900s. She held the first women's basketball game in 1893 and continued to support the sport as chairperson of the U.S. Women's Basketball Committee until 1917. Senda was enshrined into the Basketball Hall of Fame in 1985 and is also a member of the International Jewish Sports Hall of Fame.

Nancy Lieberman-Cline was the first female player to be inducted into the Basketball Hall of Fame in 1996. Nancy had an aggressive street style that inspired generations of female point guards. She won a silver medal with the U.S. Olympic Team in 1976 and then played college ball at Old Dominion, in Virginia, where she led the team to championships in 1979 and 1980. After college, she made history by playing for a men's team in the United States Basketball League. Nancy made a comeback in 1998 to play for the WNBA's Phoenix Mercury. She played for a season, then became the general manager of the Detroit Shock until 2000.

BOXING

BENNY LEONARD

Born: April 7, 1896, New York, NY
Died: April 18, 1947

[Benny] has done more to conquer anti-Semitism than a thousand textbooks.

—*writer Arthur Brisbane on Benny Leonard*

Benny Leonard trains for his difficult comeback fight with Jimmy McLarnin, October 4, 1932.

In the early twentieth century, nearly every young Jewish athlete wanted to be a professional prizefighter. Jewish boxers reigned in the professional ranks, and Jewish neighborhoods were brimming with aspiring champs. One of the best of these athletes was Benjamin Leiner, better known as Benny Leonard. From 1912 to 1932, the Great Bennah, as he was often called by his fans, had just one loss and is considered one of the best lightweight fighters who ever lived. He shined as a much-needed hero during times of discrimination for Jewish Americans and made every kid want to bob and weave just like him.

Benny Leonard was born to Orthodox parents in a rough neighborhood in New York in 1896. His parents, Gershon and Minnie Leiner, raised him on sweatshop wages and hoped he would lead a respectable and traditional Orthodox life. With all the fighting in the streets and settlement houses in his community, Benny soon took up boxing to defend himself. He was a natural at the sport, and attended a boxing club secretly on Saturdays to sharpen his skills. Benjamin first entered the ring when he was only 15 but used the name Benny Leonard so his mother would not get word of his fighting. Minnie was constantly worried for her son and considered violent sports to be against the Jewish tradition. But Benny was convinced he had a future in boxing, and nothing could keep him from the ring.

Early on, Benny received a black eye in a match and was forced to tell his parents the truth. Minnie was heartbroken, and Benny's father was concerned. When Benny gave them his $20 purse, however, his father saw the situation differently, as he had to work all week for that kind of money. He looked at the $20 and said, "All right Benny, keep on fighting. It's worth getting a black eye for $20; I am getting verschwartzt [blackened] for $20 a week."

Soon after, Benny became a rising star in the professional boxing world. Because of his strict attention to defense, he hardly ever got hurt. In fact, a popular legend is that Benny plastered his thick black hair down and dared his opponents to muss it. If his opponent touched his slick hairdo, the Great Bennah would fly into a rage and knock him out. Whether or not the myth is true, Benny suffered only five losses in his career and won 69 of his 85 total wins by knockout. He didn't give many opponents the chance to even touch his famous locks.

Benny's first big bout came in 1915 against Johnny Dundee, who was known for being both tough and clever. The fight went a fierce 10 rounds but ended in a no decision. Although he didn't defeat Dundee, Benny proved he could trade blows with the best in the division. He began to face tougher competition. Later in 1915, Benny fought world featherweight champion Johnny Kilbane. Again the fight ended in a no decision. In 1916 he challenged the world lightweight champion, Freddie Welsh, and pounded through two more no decisions. The important fights were ending uneventfully, but Benny was performing well. It was only a matter of time before he got his first big knockout.

That event came on May 28, 1917, in New York City. After the two no decision fights against Freddie Welsh, a deciding third match, or "rubber match," was scheduled. Benny came out firing, dominating the match from the first punch. He dragged Welsh through nine hammering rounds before knocking the champion out cold on the mat. The Great Bennah became the lightweight champion of the world, a title he would hold for more than seven years.

Two months later, Benny leveled Johnny Kilbane in the third round of their rematch. In 1919 Benny knocked out former lightweight champion Willie Ritchie in the eighth round. And in 1920, he defended his title against Charley White, a quick boxer known for his left hook. Benny knocked him out in the ninth before White could throw the patented punch. Benny was on a roll. He was unbeatable in the ring and drew crowds of up to 60,000 people to watch him defend his title. Writer Al Lurie called him, "the most famous Jew in the world."

Not only was Benny an incredible boxer, he was a legitimate hero, a symbol of the strength and determination for his people. At the time when Benny fought, many Jews were recent immigrants without much money. Like Benny's family, many lived in cramped homes on New York's Lower East Side and faced discrimination and low wages. Benny's successes made them feel good. Benny was giving a good name to all of American Jewry and helping them be accepted. He had flourished in a popular American sport and had proved that Jews were as capable of athletic talent and success as anyone else.

As his celebrity status grew, so did Benny's win column. He defended his title in 1922, knocking out the powerful, scrappy battler Rocky Kansas in eight rounds. In 1923 Benny fought Lew Tendler, one of the hardest punchers in the lightweight division, at Yankee Stadium in front of an enormous crowd. The fight lasted 15 rounds, but Benny emerged the victor to the roar of his hometown fans. Then, surprising many, Benny only fought twice more before retiring in 1925. His mother was ill, and Benny retired as a promise to her. "My love for her," Benny told reporters, "is greater than my love for the game." Even after her son was a millionaire and prizefighting legend, Minnie Leiner still worried for Benny's safety.

After the stock market crash in 1929, Benny returned for a brief comeback to make some money. He won 19 fights but was knocked out in his last match by the young slammer Jimmy McLarnin. Benny then realized he was no longer in his prime and decided to retire for good. Over the next few years, he taught boxing and refereed big matches for the new generation of hotshot fighters. In 1947 he died tragically, suffering a heart attack while refereeing a match at St. Nicholas Arena in New York.

He was mourned by a legion of loyal fans. Many who grieved were young men who had worshiped Benny growing up and had studied his every fight with obsessive detail. Budd Shulberg, a young fan of Benny's who later became a sportswriter, wrote in *Ring* magazine, "Babe Ruth could hit fifty-four homers that year and I didn't really care. Not even the legendary Ty Cobb brought a chill to my skin . . . that sensation was reserved for Benny Leonard." The Great Bennah gave hope to many young Jews in rough communities and was a true people's champion. He was inducted into the International Boxing Hall of Fame in 1990.

BARNEY ROSS

Born: December 23, 1909, New York, NY
Died: January 17, 1967

Barney Ross was a symbol of the Jewish people in those days in that if he could do it then we can do it.

—*ring announcer Ben Bentley*

Lightweight champ Barney Ross smiles after his workout on May 14, 1934, in training to face welterweight champ Jimmy McLarnin.

To call Barney Ross a great boxer would be too simplistic. Some athletes, like Barney, rise above their sport and also deserve to be remembered as heroic people. The record books will always tell the story of Barney's world titles and 81 professional bouts in which he was never once knocked out, but that is only half of his legacy. The other half is about a man who fought great adversity both in World War II and in his life outside the ring. Barney's story is one of dazzling sports ability combined with personal struggle and bravery. He was a man born to fight in every sense of the word.

Born in New York City to an Orthodox family, Barney was named Barnet David Rasofsky. He was a scholarly young man growing up, and his first dream was to teach Hebrew. His father, Isidore, was a rabbi and did everything to nourish the religious interests of his son. Isidore considered athletics, especially fighting, to be against God's law and discouraged Barney from competition. "Anyone who got in a fist fight," recalled Barney about his father's views, "was a tramp or a bum." Barney seemed to be on track for a traditional and spiritual career until tragedy struck his family.

Two years after Barney was born, his father decided to move the family to the west side of Chicago. Once there, he hoped to make more money operating a small grocery and dairy store. The venture was successful for a while, but it ended in unforeseen sorrow. On a cold December day in 1924, Barney's father let some strange men into the store to warm themselves by the stove and was shot to death in a panicked holdup.

In a strange twist of fate, it was his father's death that led Barney to a career in boxing. After the tragedy, Barney's mother had a nervous breakdown, and his younger siblings were placed in a Jewish orphanage. It became Barney's only wish to bring the family back together. He knew he could not do this with religious study. He needed to make money. A renowned neighborhood scrapper in his adolescence, the 14-year-old Barney picked up a pair of boxing gloves and began to practice.

In 1926, just before his 18th birthday, Barnet Rasofsky entered the New York Golden Gloves tournament under the name Barney Ross. Amazingly, he won the tournament and the featherweight title, surprising both Barney and his opponents. After some encouragement from Jackie Fields, another Jewish boxer, Barney turned professional and began learning the science of boxing.

His first professional fight came on September 1, 1929, in Los Angeles. Barney rolled through the bout, defeating Ramon Lugo in six rounds. He showed great promise in the match, using "Bennah"-like defense and perfectly timed punches, deftly handling his opponent. But no one would have guessed that Barney would go on to win 38 of his next 42 professional fights. He became a local favorite in Chicago, battling constantly and slowly making his way to the top. By 1933 Barney had earned a shot for both the lightweight and junior welterweight titles.

Tony Canzoneri held both titles, and Barney happily agreed to fight him in Chicago on June 23, 1933, in front of 13,000 fans. Barney won the fight by decision, confirming his unquestionable talent to the entire city. After the fight, Barney said, "My greatest ambition is to see to it that my mother, and the rest of her family, have everything they want." Well on his way as the defender of two world titles, Barney walked his mother home that night to an apartment filled with a reunited family.

In 1934 Barney moved up in weight class and challenged the great Jimmy McLarnin, who had beaten Benny Leonard in the Great Bennah's final fight, for the welterweight championship. Barney won the contest in front of 45,000 fans at New York's Long Island Bowl, becoming the first boxer to hold three titles simultaneously.

Barney retired in 1938 with an astounding record of 72 wins out of 81 bouts. He had 22 knockouts and only four losses. For many, this would have been enough excitement for two lifetimes, but Barney still had work to do. He enlisted in the Marine Corps after the 1941 Japanese attack on Pearl Harbor and fought in the Battle of Guadalcanal in November 1942. Barney saved the lives of three men in the battle and became one of World War II's heroes. Sportswriters across the nation praised his courage.

Barney Ross died a champion and a decorated soldier on January 17, 1967. He had been inducted into the Boxing Hall of Fame in 1956 and the International Boxing Hall of Fame in 1990. Originally called the "West Side Jewish Kid" by writers at the beginning of his career, Barney had become a legend. He took over where Benny Leonard left off, serving as a role model for his old neighborhood and for Jews all over the country. Barney was a leader and a giver and one of the most courageous athletes in the history of sports.

"SLAPSIE" MAXIE ROSENBLOOM

Born: September 6, 1904, New York, NY
Died: March 6, 1976

In my scheme of things, Slapsie Maxie Rosenbloom was a more miraculous Jewish phenomena by far than Dr. Albert Einstein.

—author Phillip Roth

Boxer-turned-actor, "Slapsie" Maxie Rosenbloom performs at the Orpheus Cafe Revue in Hollywood, 1935.

Another legendary fighter and powerful symbol of Jewish athleticism was "Slapsie" Maxie Rosenbloom. Although Maxie did not have the natural talent of Benny Leonard or Barney Ross, he was a vibrant boxing celebrity and timely fighter during an intense period of anti-Semitism. Both a great brawler and an engaging personality, Maxie won 210 career fights and appeared in more than 100 Hollywood films after his retirement from the ring. But the most important event in forming his legend was his victory over German champion Adolph Heuser two months after Hitler became chancellor of Germany. The fight played an important part in Hitler's decision to prohibit German athletes from competing against Jews, and it lifted Maxie to instant hero status among Jews and patriots alike.

Maxie grew up a troubled kid on New York's Lower East Side. A dropout and a reform school veteran, he had a reputation as a troublemaker. Maxie seemed to be involved in every fight in the neighborhood, and most of the time, he was the last one standing when the final punch was thrown. It wasn't until he was noticed fighting in the street by actor George Raft that Maxie's life began to take direction. Raft, a popular figure at the time, encouraged the young tough guy to refine his skills and become a boxer. Soon after their talk, Maxie went into training.

He first entered the ring in 1923 as a middleweight at age 19. He fought five bouts that year—all victories. After this fantastic start, Maxie upped his pace considerably, and by 1925, he had fought in 46 professional contests with only four losses. Maxie was a tough fighter, but he learned as he continued to battle that he was not the hardest hitter in his division. Maxie began developing the signature hit-and-run style that would make him famous.

Maxie realized that he could fight with greater success by taking advantage of his quickness. He would dodge around the ring throwing rapid punches. Sometimes he would punch so fast he didn't have time to make a fist and his open glove would slap his opponent across the jaw. Journalist Damon Runyon, who enjoyed writing about Maxie's vivacious ring antics, gave him the nickname "Slapsie" Maxie, and it stuck throughout his career.

By the end of 1925, "Slapsie" Maxie had earned a number 10 ranking in his division. He set his eye on the light heavyweight title and began fighting as much as possible to prepare. Maxie's defense kept him away from injury, and as the next few years passed, he perfected his swift punching approach to the game. During this time, he defeated future Hall of Famer Jack McVey and the infamous Ted "Kid" Lewis, among many others. After losing two shots at the title against champion Jimmy Slattery, he earned another chance in 1930.

Maxie made the most of this opportunity, taking the fight 15 rounds and defeating Slattery. The New York State Athletic Commission recognized him as the light heavyweight champion of the world. He was acclaimed the undisputed champion in 1932, after defeating National Boxing Association champion Lou Scozza. "Slapsie" Maxie held his title until

1934, and during that time, he fought the most of any title-holder in boxing history. Between 1930 and 1934, he fought 106 times, eight of which were title defenses. But out of all these fights, one bout carried a special historical significance long after the match was over.

In 1933 Maxie defended his title against the German bruiser Adolph Heuser. The fight was an important one for Jewish fans, particularly, as Hitler had just come to power in Germany and had been declaring Jews as feeble and second-class citizens. Hitler claimed that Aryan non-Jewish Germans were the master race and the best and strongest people in the world. Maxie's 15-round triumph over Heuser was an embarrassment to Hitler and his Nazi Party. After the fight, Hitler would not allow Germans to compete against Jews. Many believed his decision was because of Maxie's historic win.

After the big win, Maxie defended his title for another year, before losing it to Bob Olin in a controversial defeat. Many spectators at ringside felt that "Slapsie" Maxie had earned the decision, but the ruling was final. Maxie retired in 1939, having fought nearly 300 professional fights.

After boxing, Maxie let his lively personality take over and became a star of film and radio. He was loved and idolized the country over for his sense of humor and charm. "Slapsie" Maxie died in 1976, a hero to many who followed his career. He had made it from the halls of reform school to the pages of history and was inducted into the Boxing Hall of Fame, the International Boxing Hall of Fame, and the Jewish Sports Hall of Fame.

MORE JEWISH BOXERS:

Another Hall of Famer competing in the prime of Jewish boxing was hard-hitting southpaw **Lew Tendler.** Lew was a lightweight and earned 37 of his 59 career wins by knockouts.

Many believe he would have been a lightweight champion if he had not had to face Benny Leonard in two memorable fights. The first was in July of 1922. Lew managed to knock Benny down in the eighth round but could not knock him out, and the fight ended in a no decision. When the rematch came along, Benny fought more conservatively and held on to win a 15-round decision. Despite his inability to capture the lightweight title, Lew Tendler is remembered as one of the best club fighters of his day. He fought unforgettable bouts against champions and never feared an opponent, no matter how tough or reputable.

Max Baer, *left*, fights Joe Louis, just after rising from an eight-count knockdown, September 24, 1935.

Max Baer is often acknowledged as the "first Jewish heavyweight champion of the world," despite the fact that his faith was in question. Max was the son of a Scotch-Irish mother and a father who claimed a Jewish history. In spite of the criticism that Max was not a "real Jew," he thought of himself as Jewish and fought with a Star of David on his trunks. Max was an important symbol in a time when Hitler was calling the Jews a weak and inferior people. Many Jewish boxing fans saw the heavyweight title as the strongest title in all of sports. They were happy to call Max one of their own. Max commented once, "I am Jewish if I am anything at all." Whether or not this was true, everyone agreed that he was a stupendous boxer and a much-needed ally of Jews in a difficult time. In 1933, as the forces of Nazi Germany were on the rise, Max fought the German slugger, Max Schmeling. Baer hammered Schmeling before 60,000 fans in Yankee Stadium. The referee stopped the fight in the tenth round, giving Baer the victory. Max Baer went on to earn the heavyweight title in 1934.

Mike Rossman was the first Jewish champion in nearly forty years, when he won the light heavyweight championship in 1978. The son of a Jewish mother and an Italian father, Mike was born July 1, 1955. He turned professional in 1973 and fought 42 times before receiving his title shot against Victor Galindez. Mike won the bout in 13 rounds by technical knockout (three knockdowns in one round). Later in 1978, he defended his title against Aldo Traversaro with a sixth-round technical knockout. He finished his career in 1983, with 44 wins, seven losses, and three draws. Twenty-seven of his wins were earned by knockout.

Dana Rosenblatt was a super middleweight who has won three versions of the world title. Rosenblatt boxes with a Star of David on his trunks. He retired in 2003 with an outstanding 37–1–2 record. **Yuri Foreman** is a super welterweight with a 17–0 record as of June 2003. He also wore a Star of David on his trunks. His amateur record was 75–5.

FOOTBALL

SID LUCKMAN

Born: November 21, 1916, Brooklyn, NY
Died: July 5, 1998.

Sid made himself a great quarterback. No one else did it for him.

—*Chicago Bears coach George Halas on Sid Luckman*

Sid Luckman prepares to pass, September 1948.

Sid Luckman is considered one of the most influential quarterbacks to ever play the game of football. Leading the Chicago Bears through a decade of dominance in the 1940s, Sid mastered the T-formation offense and helped reinvent the passing game. He wasn't always the quickest player on the field, and he wasn't often able to pass the longest. But Sid was the smartest. He had fantastic awareness on the field and was an escape artist when it came to dodging the rush. He was also a great defensive back and punter in an era when players often did not specialize in one position. His skills at quarterback, however, are what made him a legend. In a time when the pass-oriented offense was still developing, Sid set records that remain unbroken to this day.

Born in Brooklyn, New York, on November 21, 1916, Sid Luckman was drawn to sports at an early age. Throughout his childhood, Sid could always be found with a ball in his hands. Depending on the season, he tossed a baseball or a football, acting out big games in his head. It was no surprise to anyone when Sid tried out for the football squad in high school. He made the junior varsity team at Erasmus High School in Brooklyn when he was only a freshman, and by the following season, he had become quarterback of the varsity team. The team came together under Sid's leadership, and before he graduated, Sid led Erasmus to a borough championship.

Sid's next stop was college ball at Columbia University. He was a great prospect for the Columbia Lions football team, but some of the coaches wondered how his game would hold up in the fast-paced world of college football. That question was answered in Sid's first game. He ran for a touchdown, tossed a touchdown pass, and threw another 33-yard bomb that resulted in a quick score. Playing against Army during his sophomore year, Sid almost single-handedly won the game. He passed, ran, punted, tackled, and blocked. After the game his coach, Lou Little, said, "He's only a sophomore, but I think he's one of the best passers in the game right now. He's the best I ever had."

Sid was a remarkable player, but the Lions were not a great team. Game after game, Sid amazed the crowds with his accurate passing and deft maneuvering on the field. The *New York Times* wrote about him after a loss to Navy, saying, "Once more, Columbia's star [quarterback], Sid Luckman, covered himself with glory. Although his cause was the losing one, the sharpshooting Lion ace was easily the outstanding player on the field." Famous sportswriter Jon Kieran wrote about a game in Sid's senior year against Yale. He said, "[Sid] did everything for Columbia except lead the band between halves."

After winning praise at Columbia, Sid got his chance to play professional football when the Chicago Bears drafted him. Chicago coach George Halas thought Sid would be perfect to lead his T-formation offense and did everything possible to secure him for the Bears. Sid joined the team in 1939, but he would have to prove himself again before he earned the position of starting quarterback. Sid got his chance in mid-October of his first season.

The Bears were down 16–0 to the New York Giants, and Halas decided to give his starter a rest. Sid came in off the bench and immediately set out to show his stuff. Just after entering the game, he connected on a 68-yard touchdown pass, stunning the crowd and the Giants alike. The Bears stopped the Giants on defense, and again Luckman moved the Bears up and down the field with lightning speed. He started on his own 25-yard line and took the team in for another score. The Bears lost the game 16–13, but the 58,000 fans went wild for Sid's gutsy comeback. It was clear that a professional star had been born.

In his next season, Sid slowly began creating a place for himself as one of the greatest quarterbacks of his time. Week in and week out, he threw dazzling passes and called one smart play after another. The Bears won the championship that season 73–0 against the Redskins in the most lopsided championship game in professional football history. Just weeks before, the Redskins had completely shut down the Bears' offense in a 7–3 victory. This made their humiliating defeat even more incredible. The game highlighted Sid's mastery of offensive strategy. There wasn't a moment of the championship game that Sid and the Bears did not dominate. The *New York Times* said of Sid's performance, "no field general ever called plays more artistically or engineered a touchdown parade in a more letter-perfect fashion."

The Bears won the championship again in 1941 with Sid at the helm, defeating the Giants 34–9. They had a perfect regular season record in 1942 but lost to the Redskins in the championship game. The year 1943 was one of Sid's best seasons. He was league MVP and threw for a record 28 touchdowns in only 10 games. (This record stood until 1959, when Johnny Unitas threw 32 touchdowns.) On November 14, 1943, Sid completed 23 passes out of 30 attempts, passing for 443 yards and seven touchdowns. In the championship game, Sid threw for 286 yards and five touchdowns. In 1946 Sid led the Bears to their fourth championship in seven years.

Sid slowed down a bit during his last four seasons but still led the Bears to a second-place finish every year. He retired in 1950 with 14,683 passing yards in 128 professional games. This number, along with his 137 passing touchdowns, remains a Bears' franchise record. In 1965 Sid became only the second quarterback to be inducted into the Pro Football Hall of Fame. He is also a member of the International Jewish Sports Hall of Fame. Many consider Sid one of the architects of the modern passing offense and one of the best quarterbacks to ever take the field.

RON MIX

Born: March 10, 1938, Los Angeles, CA

When you're running behind Mix, it's like you're a little kid and he's your big brother protecting you from the wolves.

—*Chargers running back*
Paul Lowe on Ron Mix

Ron Mix in his Chargers uniform, August 1963

Being a lineman is often a thankless job. During a game, most fans concentrate on the backfield action, watching the quarterback and hoping for big plays. For a few years, Ron Mix managed to capture the attention of fans as one of the most exciting offensive linemen to ever don a uniform. Ron was a beast on the field, taking out the defense two and three men at a time and clearing a path for the offense. He won nearly every honor possible at his position, including nine All Pro citations. (He played in eight Pro Bowls.) Ron brought respect to the unsung positions in the game with his overwhelming power and athleticism. His career was an inspiration to football's hardworking big men.

Born Ronald Jack Mix on March 10, 1938, Ron grew up in Los Angeles, California, and attended the University of Southern California (USC) on a football scholarship. Because of his excellence in academics as well as his ferocity on the gridiron, Ron was nicknamed the Intellectual Assassin. He was brilliant in both arenas and was famous for his constant drive to better himself. Ron entered USC as a freshman weighing 180 pounds but left the school nearing 250 pounds. According to his teammates, the industrious young player never seemed to leave the gym.

Ron became a starting lineman at USC his sophomore year and held onto his position for three years. He was voted team captain during the 1959 season, when the USC Trojans tied for first place in the Pacific Coast Conference with a record of 8–2–0. Ranked fourteenth in the nation that season, Ron's team did not play in the postseason as the result of an earlier NCAA ban. Even though the ban was disappointing, Ron's personal accolades helped ease the pain. He was named first team All-American, AP All-Pacific Coast first team, All Big Five first team, and won the USC Lineman Award.

In 1960 Ron was drafted by both the American Football League (AFL) and the National Football League (NFL). The Baltimore Colts wanted him for the NFL, and the Boston (later New England) Patriots and Los Angeles Chargers sought him for the AFL. Even though the AFL was a newly formed league, Ron chose to play in Los Angeles. Ron said about the choice, "The Colts offered me $8,500 to come play in cold Baltimore. The Chargers offered me $12,000 to play in my hometown. It was one of my easier decisions."

Ron soon became the best lineman in the upstart league. He had superior fundamentals and quickly put them to use in the AFL. With so many big players in the league, Ron could not rely solely on his size to get by. He once said, "With a man outweighing you by anywhere from 10 to 50 to 60 pounds, you have to use a lot of technique blocks. You're not going to be able to drive a man out by force and overpower him like you did in college." Nevertheless, when Ron had a size advantage, he used it, knocking defenders out of the way left and right to protect his quarterback or runners. Behind his masterful pass protection, the Chargers made the AFL Championship Game in Ron's first season, losing to the Houston Oilers 26–17. The loss was a disappointing one, but the season had been a brilliant success for the rookie lineman.

In 1961 the now San Diego Chargers achieved a record of 12–2–0. They returned to the championship game but lost again to the Houston Oilers. It wasn't until 1963 that Ron's Chargers proved that they were the best in the AFL. They made the championship game for the third time and defeated the Patriots 51–10. Ron was the hero of the game, making a series of incredible plays. On one occasion, he blocked three separate Patriots players to shield a touchdown run. *Newsweek* wrote about the game, "Mix is not only the best offensive lineman in the AFL, he is also a performer with enough dash to draw one eye of the spectator away from the glamour of the backfield."

Ron played with the San Diego Chargers until 1970. He took them to two more AFL Championship Games before retiring. He came out of retirement to play with the Oakland Raiders in 1971 but then retired again after the season. When he quit the game, coaches and players lauded Ron as the best offensive lineman. The "Intellectual Assassin" always had a finely crafted quote for the media. He talked about his love for studying and spoke on occasion about his Jewish heritage. "It would have been nice if people had said, 'There's Ron Mix, a human being who made good,'" Ron said. "But until that time in history comes around, I'm proud when they say 'There's Ron Mix, a Jewish football player who made good.'"

Ron was unanimously voted to the All-Time AFL Team by the Pro Football Hall of Fame in 1969. He was only the sixth lineman to receive this honor. He is also a member of the International Jewish Sports Hall of Fame and the USC Athletic Hall of Fame. He played in seven All-Star games and, incredibly, was only called for holding twice in his entire career. Longtime Jewish coach Sid Gillman said of Ron, "Ron Mix is one of the greats of all time. I think he's the greatest tackle who ever lived."

JAY FIEDLER

Jay Fiedler looks for the receiver, October 21, 2002.

Born: December 29, 1971, Oceanside, NY

All along I just kept saying to myself if I just got a chance to prove to everyone I can play, then I can stick around.

—Jay Fiedler to the Jewish Post, June 2000

Jay Fiedler is a talented quarterback in the NFL. His career record, an impressive 36–17 after the 2003 season, is one of the best among active quarterbacks. He is the fifth fastest quarterback in history to reach 25 wins. With numbers like these, Jewish sports fans have begun to draw comparisons to the great Sid Luckman. Jay once made 92 straight pass attempts without an interception, and he also has great skill at rushing the ball. Jay seems to get better every season, and with a lengthy contract in place, Miami Dolphins' fans can expect more excitement from this backfield ace.

Growing up in Oceanside, New York, Jay was a multitalented athlete. He lettered in football, baseball, and track while attending Oceanside High School and received the Scholar-Athlete Award from the National Football Foundation and Hall of Fame in 1989. As a testament to his combined scholarly and athletic talents, Jay chose to go to college at an Ivy League school, Dartmouth College. His ability was soon apparent to the Dartmouth coach, and Jay became a starter for the last three years of his college career. His performance on the field was nothing short of astounding. Jay set four school passing records with 456 completions, 813 attempts, 6,684 total yards, and an incredible 58 touchdowns. He earned first-team All-Ivy League honors in both his junior (1992) and senior (1993) years.

When it came time to go pro in 1994, Jay signed with the Philadelphia Eagles as an undrafted rookie. He wasn't sure how much playing time he would get coming out of the Ivy League, but he suited up as a third-string quarterback and patiently waited for his chance. That chance would not come for a while. Jay was passed around to different teams in the NFL and World League over the next few years and did not see much playing time until signing with the Jacksonville Jaguars in 1999. Jay came in for injured Mark Brunell in an October game and brought the Jags back to win from a 7–6 deficit. His first start came in January against the Bengals, and Jay made it count. He connected on 28 of 39 passes for 317 yards with one touchdown and no interceptions. The Jaguars won the game, and Jay won the respect he deserved.

Jay Fiedler signed with the Miami Dolphins in 2000. He started 15 games that year and finished the season having completed 204 of 357 passes with 2,402 total passing yards and 14 touchdowns. He also finished second on the Dolphins in rushing, with 267 yards and one rushing touchdown. He went 10–5 as a starter and led the Dolphins to the postseason. They won the American Football Conference (AFC) Wild Card game against the Colts but lost the following week against the Oakland Raiders. Despite the loss, the season was considered a great success. Jay had finally found his home in professional football.

In 2001 Jay was re-signed to a five-year contract through 2006. He started all 16 regular season games in 2001 and finished with 3,290 yards and 20 touchdowns. Jay became the second quarterback in Dolphins history (the other was Dan Marino) to throw over 3,000 yards in a season. Jay also increased his rushing yards to 321. But perhaps the most impressive statistic is that Jay led his team to fourth-quarter comebacks five times in the 2001 season. The Dolphins made the playoffs again but lost in the first round to the eventual Super Bowl champions, the Baltimore Ravens.

Jay met with an unfortunate injury in the 2002 season but still got a chance to prove himself as the leader of the team. In the first six games of the season, Jay had led the team to a 5–1 record, first place in the AFC East. He was on pace for more personal and team records when he broke his thumb on his throwing hand in a mid-October game against the Denver Broncos. It was incredibly painful, but he stayed in the close game and led his team down the field for a winning field goal. "He wanted to see this thing through," said Miami coach Dave Wannstedt. Fortunately for the Dolphins, Jay has had surgery on the thumb and has returned to the game.

Jay is loved not only by Dolphins fans but also throughout the NFL. His actions on and off the gridiron are selfless and admirable. Aside from giving his all to his team on game day, Jay also gives his time to Habitat for Humanity, Boys and Girls Clubs, and the Reach for the Stars Foundation, which benefits children with cystic fibrosis. Besides his induction into the International Jewish Sports Hall of Fame, he has been honored with the Dick Steinberg Good Guy Award. The New York Jewish Sports Hall of Fame gives the award annually to an athlete who symbolizes the good aspects of competitive sports. The sky is the limit for Jay Fiedler. His character and talent drives him to be the best.

MORE JEWISH FOOTBALL STARS:

Benny Friedman was a spectacular Jewish quarterback in the late 1920s and early 1930s. He was a two-time All-American quarterback and halfback at the University of Michigan before moving to the NFL. The only player in football history to lead the NFL in passing and rushing yards, Benny was unpredictable on the field. He could throw the long bomb or take off running on any down. Often called the best player not in the Hall of Fame, Benny is credited with paving the way for great passers from Sid Luckman to Michael Vick.

Marshall Goldberg, nicknamed Biggie because he played football with older kids when he was young, was a renowned player at two positions in the late 1930s and early 1940s. Marshall could play running back and was said to have "natural instincts" as a defensive back. He could blaze across the open field on one play and throw a bone-crushing block on the next. He set new rushing records playing college ball at the University of Pittsburgh, then made the professional ranks in 1939. At different times in his career, Marshall led the NFL in interceptions and kickoff returns. He was inducted into the College Football Hall of Fame in 1958.

Some of the other players in the NFL include **Mike Rosenthal**, offensive tackle with the Minnesota Vikings, an All-American at Notre Dame in 1998 who spent several years with the New York Giants. **Josh Miller** is an outstanding punter for the Pittsburgh Steelers, where he has played since 1996 following an All-American career at the University of Arizona. **Josh Taves** is a defensive lineman who played with the Oakland Raiders in 2000–2001 and the Carolina Panthers in 2003. **Lennie Friedman**, an offensive guard, was an All-Atlantic Coast Conference selection at Duke University, was drafted in the second round by the Denver Broncos, and was playing for the Washington Redskins in 2003.

HOCKEY

JEFF HALPERN

Born: May 3, 1976,
Potomac, MD

On Saturday night, I'd
rather be playing a game
than going to a party.

*—Jeff Halpern
on his childhood obsession
with hockey*

One of the best defensive centers in professional hockey, Jeff Halpern is a rising star for the Washington Capitals. He has a fantastic overall game and amazes fans with his combination of scoring and penalty killing.

Jeff Halpern, playing for the Capitals, has been skating since age three.

Coming from Maryland, a state that has sent only three players to the National Hockey League (NHL), Jeff fought against tough odds to make it as a professional hockey player. He always believed he could succeed on the ice.

"I suppose I was there when I was a newborn," says Jeff about attending Capitals' games when he was young. Born in Potomac, Maryland, a suburb of Washington, D.C., Jeff's parents took him to countless games when he was young. "I have a collection of memories," he says, "racing over to the games with my family." Jeff's father, Mel Halpern, started Jeff skating at the age of three and enrolled him in a hockey clinic when he was four. By the time Jeff was six, he was already on a traveling team.

At the young age of nine, Jeff made the local All-Star team called the Little Caps. Most of his teammates were eleven or twelve years old, but Jeff's natural talent for the sport helped him make the cut. Then serious traveling began. The Little Caps played in tournaments across the Northeast and into Canada, and Mel drove Jeff to every one in his Dodge minivan. As Jeff got older, his father would drive him to Connecticut for a practice, returning home the same night. "My dad didn't mind the driving," said Jeff. "He loved hockey."

When high school rolled around, Jeff and his parents realized his local high school didn't have a hockey team. Although it was a financial sacrifice for Jeff's family, they happily sent him to a private school in New Hampshire that had an excellent hockey program. Jeff played well at his new high school, but he received little interest from Division I colleges. Jeff took a risk and decided to move to Canada and play for the Stratford Cullitons. Jeff exploded on the ice, scoring 48 goals and 96 assists in a 72-game season. He led the Cullitons to a league championship, and suddenly every Ivy League school in the USA wanted Jeff Halpern.

Jeff chose Princeton and almost immediately became a college hockey star. He played varsity hockey from 1995 to 1999. In his junior year, he had 28 goals and 25 assists in 36 games. "That was a breakout year for me," Jeff says, "and I started getting attention." In his senior year, Jeff led Princeton to the most wins in school history and won the school's Roper Trophy for athletic and academic achievement. The NHL teams started calling, and by the end of his senior season, Jeff had signed with his hometown Capitals.

In 1999–2000, his rookie season for the Capitals, Jeff scored 18 goals and passed for 11 assists. He ranked first on the team in shorthanded goals with four. He was named NHL rookie of the month in March after scoring eight goals. But the 2000–2001 season was Jeff's standout season in the pros. He scored 21 goals and had 21 assists. He finished third on the team in goals and ranked first on the team in game-tying goals with five. Unfortunately, Jeff sustained a knee injury in the 2001–2002 season and sat out the last 34 games of the year. He managed to score five goals and 14 assists before the injury on January 16, 2002, but was frustrated with his condition.

Jeff rebounded in the 2002–2003 season with 13 goals and 21 assists, but he is still not back to playing as he did in 2000–2001. Fortunately for the Jewish star, he is young and has plenty of time to reestablish his reputation for scoring in the NHL. Capitals's fans expect spectacular things from their hometown boy in the years to come. He is proof that anyone can chase down a dream with enough effort and determination, even a hockey player from Maryland.

MORE JEWISH HOCKEY STARS:

Mathieu Schneider has been an outstanding defenseman in the NHL since 1987. He played most of his career for the Montreal Canadians and is currently skating for the Detroit Red Wings. Through 2002 he had scored 506 points on 154 goals and 352 assists. He has been an All Star two times and got two assists in the 2002 All Star Game. He also was a Stanley Cup winner with Montreal and played on the 1998 U.S. Olympic Hockey team. Other promising young hockey players are **Steve Dubinsky**, who has played with three NHL teams, and **Max Birbraer** drafted by the New Jersey Devils.

OLYMPICS

FEMALE ATHLETES

KERRI STRUG

Born: November 19, 1977, Tucson, AZ

She has been the ultimate team player, often sacrificing her own goals to advance those of USA gymnastics.

—gold-medal-winning gymnast Mary Lou Retton on Kerri Strug

Kerri Strug performs on the balance beam.

Many people view the Olympic Games as the most important competition in the world of sports. Olympic participants in the Games train for years with hope of winning a gold medal for their country. Pressure is high. The whole world watches. Athletes can become heroes in a matter of moments. Only a lucky few actually make it to the top. Jewish gymnast Kerri Strug is one such athlete. She took the Olympic world by storm in 1996 by vaulting on an injured ankle to bring the U.S. Gymnastics team their first-ever gold medal in team competition. Her courage was widely celebrated, and the event lives on as one of the most exciting in Olympic history.

Kerri was born November 19, 1977, in Tucson, Arizona. She started gymnastics in 1982, when she was just five years old. Her older sister was a gymnast, and Kerri wanted to be just like her. By the late 1980s, Kerri was one of the top up-and-coming gymnasts in the country. As she got older, Kerri had to decide how serious she was about the sport. To train for the Olympics, she would need a good coach. In 1991, when she was only 13, Kerri left her home in Tucson to train with the famous coach, Bela Karolyi. She competed in the 1991 U.S. Championships and finished first in the vault and third all-around. After the competition, Kerri was chosen for the national team. Later that year, at the World Championships, Kerri earned a silver medal in the team overall competition.

In 1992 Kerri competed in her first Olympic Games in Barcelona, Spain. At 14, she was the youngest U.S. athlete competing in any sport. This did not stop her from making her presence known at the Games. Kerri won a bronze medal in the team combined exercises and finished fourteenth in the world in the individual all-around. This was an impressive feat, but Kerri was still young and had plenty of time to keep training. Her coaches believed she had unlimited potential.

Kerri continued competing with the national team after the 1992 Games, accumulating awards wherever she went. She won a silver medal at the 1994 World Championships. In 1995 she won the individual all-around competition at the U.S. Olympic Festival. None of these events were as important to Kerri and her American teammates as the upcoming 1996 Olympic Games in Atlanta. The country expected great things from the team, who would be performing in front of a frenzied home crowd.

As it turned out, 1996 would be the year that Kerri would go down in Olympic history. The U.S. team competed well and went on to the finals trailing Russia by .127 points. A nearly flawless performance on the bars propelled the team into first place, but they needed to stay sharp to cement their victory. Kerri Strug was the last competitor for the U.S. team, and she was competing in her prime event, the vault, at which she was one of the best in the world. Then misfortune struck when she fell backward on the landing of her first vault and injured her left ankle. The U.S. team already had a low vault score, and Kerri had to decide instantly if she would vault a second time.

"The moment my feet hit the floor, I heard a pop," Kerri said later about the first vault. "As I scrambled to stand, a fiery pain shot up my left leg." Still, Kerri was certain that her team would earn gold if she vaulted once more. Carefully, she limped to the start of the runway. Then to the amazement of viewers worldwide, Kerri ran down the runway, vaulted, and landed firmly on two feet. The crowd erupted in applause, and Kerri collapsed to be carried away by her coaches. She received a score of 9.71, and the U.S. team won their first gold medal in the team competition. They beat Russia and Romania by less than a point.

After this moment, Kerri was immediately transformed into a hero. She won the Olympic Spirit Award, a prize given to athletes who have overcome adversity to reach their Olympic goals. She was chosen as one of America's ten most fascinating people for a Barbara Walters television special. She appeared on the covers of *Time* and *People* magazines and made numerous guest appearances on television shows including *Saturday Night Live* and the *Tonight Show with Jay Leno*. She had inspired and captured the admiration of the United States with her daring performance. *Time* magazine wrote, "America got another electrifying moment to put in its collective sports memory bank."

When the media excitement finally died down, Kerri accepted the role of honorary captain for the 1997 U.S. team at the Maccabiah Games in Israel. She told reporters that the event was a chance "to get back with my culture and heritage. The Jewish community has been wonderful and kind," she added. Kerri proudly carried the torch into Ramat Gan Stadium in Tel Aviv. In 2002 Kerri was inducted into the U.S. Gymnastics Hall of Fame. She is also a member of the Jewish Sports Hall of Fame. She will always be remembered for that day in Atlanta when she was a hero for her team and her country.

SASHA COHEN

Born: October 6, 1984, Westwood, CA

She's a very unique person whose talents transcend the technical elements.

—former coach John Nickson on Sasha Cohen

It is hard to think of a more popular young figure skater than Sasha Cohen. Sasha is one of the most celebrated Jewish athletes in history, and her fame continues to grow with each

Sasha Cohen performs in the 2003 World Figure Skating Championship long program.

event she skates. Ever since her breakout performance in the 2002 Olympic Games in Salt Lake City, Utah, Sasha has enjoyed a successful career of competition and celebrity status in the figure skating world. She has her eye on the 2006 Winter Games in Torino, Italy, and many believe she has a legitimate shot at the gold medal. Until that time, Sasha continues to thrill audiences with her elegant and athletic style of skating.

Alexandra Pauline Cohen, nicknamed Sasha, was born on October 6, 1984, in Westwood, California. Her parents are Galina and Roger, and she has a sister, Natasha. Her mother is of Ukrainian descent, and Sasha speaks both Russian and English, often translating for her fellow skaters at international events. Before beginning figure skating at the age of seven, Sasha practiced gymnastics and dance. She excelled in all her childhood athletic pursuits but realized early that figure skating was her passion. She began to skate seriously at the age of ten.

Soon after her decision to start intensive training, Sasha began to compete in regional events. She quickly mastered her double jumps and compiled a long list of accomplishments throughout the mid- to late 1990s. In 1996, at the age of 12, Sasha took fourth place at the Southwest Pacific Regionals, then second in 1997. By 1999 she had finished first in the Southwest Pacific Regionals and second in the U.S. Junior National Championships. Sasha was chosen for the U.S. Figure Skating Team B for the 1999–2000 season.

There was no question that Sasha was a rising star in the figure skating world. But there was a big difference between junior and senior competitions, and Sasha would have to prove herself worthy of her selection to the U.S. team. She began to set ambitious goals for herself and told *Blades on Ice* magazine that she hoped to place in the top four in the 2000 U.S. National Championships in Cleveland, Ohio. Incredibly, Sasha placed first in the short program, second in the long program, and second overall. This performance surpassed her own expectations and made her an even bigger name in the ranks of competitive skating.

Sasha missed the 2001 season with a back injury but stayed strong, rehabilitating her back every day. By 2002 she had returned more impressive than ever. She took second in the U.S. National Championships and earned a spot on the U.S. Olympic Team for the 2002 Games in Salt Lake City. "I'm looking forward to everything," she said about her selection to the Games, "Opening and closing ceremonies, staying in the village, hopefully skating my best and winning a medal." Despite a performance that the *New York Times* called "flashing," and "airtight," Sasha finished just off the medal stand in fourth place. The judging was controversial, and many people, including the *Times* reporter Selena Roberts, thought Sasha was deserving of a medal. Sasha put the disappointment behind her and set about eclipsing the competition in an astounding series of professional events.

In 2002 Sasha finished first in Skate Canada (Grand Prix), the Trophee Lalique (Grand Prix), the Sears Figure Skating Open, and the Crest Whitestrips International Figure Skating Challenge. In 2003 she took gold at the Grand Prix Final in St. Petersburg, Russia, but finished a disappointing fourth in the World Championships.

At the 2004 U.S. Figure Skating Championships, Sasha outskated Michelle Kwan by winning the short program but still placed second behind Kwan for the title. Sasha attributes this latest success to her change in coaches (from Tatiana Tarasova to Robin Wagner) just two weeks before the competition. "Robin and I have so much in common," Sasha said of her new coach. "We speak the same language. We have that chemistry. We really click. I'm having a good time on and off the ice."

Sasha is looking forward to the 2006 Winter Games and feels she is growing stronger every day. "I am being pushed farther than I ever thought possible," she says. "There is nothing more satisfying than getting off the ice and knowing you have become a better skater that day." Sasha Cohen's fans anxiously await this young superstar's appearance in the next Olympic Games.

MORE JEWISH FEMALE OLYMPIANS:

Marilyn Ramenofsky was a record-breaking Jewish Olympian in the 1960s. A swimmer, Marilyn competed in the 400-meter freestyle. She swam for the U.S. National Team at the 1964 Tokyo games and broke the Olympic record for the 400-meter freestyle with a time of 4:47.7. She managed to lower this time to 4:44.6 in the final heat but finished in second place behind teammate Virginia Duenkel. Marilyn went home with the silver medal. In 1988 she was inducted into the International Jewish Hall of Fame. Marilyn once said of her Jewish fans, "The Jewish community [always] came out of the woodwork to support me."

Sara DeCosta is another Jewish star on ice, but her sport is a little rougher than Sasha Cohen's. Sara is a gold-medal-winning goalie for the U.S. Women's Hockey Team. Her team took gold in the 1998 Winter Olympics in Nagano and silver in the 2002 Games in Salt Lake City. Sara has always been a tough competitor. She played on the boys' hockey team in high school and was even the team's MVP in 1995 and 1996. She later became the first girl to play in the Rhode Island Interscholastic League Championship Division. Sara has been a vital member of the U.S. team since 1998 and was named USA Hockey Women's Player of the Year in 2000.

OLYMPICS

MALE ATHLETES

MARK SPITZ

Born: February 10, 1950, Modesto, CA

Mark Spitz is in as complete command of his sport as any other athlete in history.

—Time *magazine,*
September 1972

Mark Spitz displays his gold medals from the Pan American Games in Winnipeg, August 2, 1967.

Olympic athletes work their entire young adult lives with the sole hope of winning gold in the revered Games. Those who stand on the podium with a gold medal around their neck, hearing their national anthem, often say that it is the single most important moment of their lives. Many times, the athletes are moved to tears by the experience. Imagine how Olympic swimmer Mark Spitz must have felt when he won seven gold medals in the 1972 Summer Olympics in Munich, Germany, and approached that podium seven separate times. Mark not only won gold medals in every event that he entered, he also set seven world records. His triumph has yet to be matched in the history of Olympic competition.

Mark Spitz was born February 10, 1950, in Modesto, California. According to his parents, Mark showed a natural talent for swimming even when he was barely able to walk. He was two when his family moved to Honolulu, and Mark's parents took him to the beaches of Waikiki nearly every day. Mark immediately fell in love with the water. "You should have seen that little boy dash into the ocean," Mark's father told *Time* magazine in 1968. At eight, Mark's family moved back to California, where he took swimming lessons at the local YMCA. By ten, Mark held seventeen national records in his age group.

By 1964 Mark had begun training under the famous coach of the Santa Clara Swim Club, George Haines. Mark qualified for the National Championships that year at age fourteen. The next year, Mark won four gold medals at the Maccabiah Games in Tel Aviv. To many it seemed that Mark was just a kid coming out of nowhere. But he pushed himself harder than the average athlete. With the support of his father, Mark was determined to be the best. When Mark missed his Hebrew lessons to practice, his father would say, "Even God likes a winner!" At times, his father was accused of pushing Mark too hard. As his father said, "You know why I pushed him? Because he was so great, that's why."

By 1967 Mark had set a new world record for the 400-meter freestyle in a California meet, then dominated the Pan American Games a month later with five gold medals. He set two more world records in the competition. Before the year ended, Mark had set another three world records and was declared Swimmer of the Year by *Swimming World* magazine.

Competitors had little hope of beating Mark Spitz at the 1968 Olympic Games in Mexico City. Mark boldly predicted that he would win six gold medals in all six of his events. He was criticized for his bravado, and many writers in the sports community felt he was being cocky, not confident. But Mark was young and riding the wave of his success. It was only after his disappointment at the Games that he began to view things more realistically. Although he did win gold in two relay events, he performed poorly in his individual events, capturing a bronze and a silver. For anyone else, this would have been a great triumph, but Mark was a record breaker and had expected to sweep the Games.

After his letdown at the 1968 Olympics, Mark enrolled at Indiana University, a school known for its unbeatable swimming program. He was more humble, and his coach urged the team not to judge Mark for his past behavior. Increasingly mature, Mark returned to a life of intense training and competing, concentrating only on his education and his sport. In 1969 he returned to the Maccabiah Games and took home six gold medals in all six of his events. He could have won a seventh, but Mark sat out his final race so a teammate could win the gold. Mark had regained his confidence and become a better person in the process.

In 1971 he again took the amateur swimming world by storm. Mark broke seven world records in the course of the year, winning four AAU Championships and two NCAA Championships. He won the *Swimming World* award again, as well as the prestigious Sullivan Award as the best amateur athlete in the country. The entire sports community waited with anticipation for the 1972 Olympic Games in Munich, Germany, to see if Mark could succeed where he had failed before.

On Monday, August 28, the first day of competition for Mark, he destroyed the world record in the 200-meter butterfly and then led the American relay team to a gold medal in the 400-meter freestyle. The relay performance was also a world record. "I feel great!" Mark said after his incredible first day. On Tuesday he won the gold in the 200-meter freestyle and set another world record. On Thursday it was gold again, as Mark set a new world record in the 100-meter butterfly. Later in the day, he led the relay team to their second gold in the 800-meter freestyle. By the end of the day, Mark had tied the record for most gold medals in a single Olympics with five. He still had two events left.

On Sunday, September 3, Mark won his sixth gold medal in his least dominant event, the 100-meter freestyle, and set another world record. The next day, in his final event of the Games, Mark won gold medal number seven with the relay team in the 400-meter medley, in which he set one last world record. He was undoubtedly the best swimmer who had ever graced the Olympic pool. The importance of a Jew succeeding in Germany was not lost on Mark. He said later in life, "I feel that being a Jewish athlete has helped our cause. We have shown that we are as good as the next guy."

However, the 1972 Olympics were bittersweet for Jewish fans. At 4:30 A.M. on September 5, Palestinian terrorists broke into the athletic compound in Munich and killed two members of the Israeli delegation. They took nine others hostage. Mark was immediately flown from the area, after briefly addressing the media. He said, "As a human being and a Jew, I am shocked and saddened by the outrageous act in the Olympic village." Tragically, the hostages were killed later in an attempted rescue. Nothing could take away Mark's amazing accomplishments, but many would remember the Games for the unspeakable catastrophe in the village.

Mark retired after the 1972 Games, but made millions from endorsements. He enjoyed his success this time with no regrets. He trained for a brief comeback for the 1992 Olympics at the age of 39 but couldn't keep up with the younger guys who swam like Mark in his prime. Mark Spitz is a member of the International Jewish Sports Hall of Fame and is remembered as the most successful single-games Olympian in history.

LENNY KRAYZELBURG

Born: September 28, 1975, Odessa, Ukraine

He's the best in the world.

—former Olympic champion John Naber on Lenny Krayzelburg

Lenny Krayzelburg swims his way to gold, Sydney, 2002.

Carrying on Mark Spitz's tradition of Olympic excellence in the swimming pool is another proud Jewish athlete, Lenny Krayzelburg. Lenny competed in the 2000 Summer Games in Sydney, Australia, and won over the crowds with his stunning speed and his powerful personality. Like Mark Spitz in his prime, Lenny took gold in every event he entered, earning two individual medals and one team medal. But Lenny's journey to the top was full of hardship, and he often thought of quitting the sport that came so naturally to him. With the support of his family, however, and a steady drive to improve, Lenny's swimming career reached dizzying heights in the 2000 Games. Lenny became a household name and a U.S. figurehead for competitive swimming.

Lenny Krayzelburg was born in 1975 in Odessa, Ukraine, which was then part of the Soviet Union. During his childhood, Lenny trained in a special sports school with 44 other talented swimmers. But daily life was often unkind to Jewish families at that time in Odessa, and Lenny's family emigrated to the United States in 1989 to escape the anti-Semitic environment and to avoid having Lenny drafted by the Soviet Union's Red Army. The Krayzelburgs moved to California, and

Lenny attended high school in Fairfax. The school did not have a swim team so Lenny had to commute to Santa Monica, where he could compete in a swim club. Lenny's poor English skills made him feel different, and he had a hard time communicating with his teammates and coach. Occasionally he thought about quitting the team, but his father would not let Lenny's dream die. "Complete your journey," his father told him. So Lenny kept with the schedule, steadily growing faster and stronger in the water.

Lenny became an American citizen in 1994. Although he had emerged as a spectacular swimming talent, he just missed making the 1996 Olympic team. The backstroke was his specialty, and by 1998 he had become the fastest backstroker in the world. He won gold medals at the World Championships in Perth, Australia, in both the 100-meter and the 200-meter backstroke. In 1999, while competing at the University of Southern California, he broke the world record in the 50-meter, the 100-meter, and the 200-meter backstroke and was voted Swimmer of the Year by USA Swimming Inc. The swimming world knew that Lenny Krayzelburg was hitting his stride.

Fortunately for Lenny, his stroke was peaking with the Olympics just around the corner. The 2000 Games would be held in Australia, and Australian fans were crazy about swimming. It was one of the premier events of the Games, and the pressure was unbelievably high. If this pressure bothered Lenny, it certainly didn't show in his performance. Lenny put on a dazzling show, breaking Olympic records in both of his backstroke events and leading the U.S. 400-meter relay team to the gold medal. Lenny received a total of three gold medals and found himself in the media spotlight as America's most successful swimmer.

His next career decision shocked many swimming fans. Lenny decided to compete in the 2001 Maccabiah Games in

Israel instead of the World Championships in Japan. The events took place at the same time, and Lenny announced his decision after the Olympics in 2000. "I have never been to Israel," said Lenny, "and I really would like to go there and compete in the Maccabiah Games next year. It is a very important part of my heritage." The media was surprised, but members of the Jewish community came out publicly to support Lenny's decision. Mark Spitz made a statement about Lenny, saying, "I think it's terrific that Lenny is choosing to swim at the Maccabiah Games. I'd like to see Lenny break one or both of his records in Israel."

On June 15, 2001, Lenny carried the American flag on behalf of the U.S. team. In his first race, Lenny broke his 100-meter backstroke record by nearly three seconds. Unfortunately, he injured his shoulder and could not swim in his other scheduled races, but the world record was a great victory for Lenny and the Maccabiah Games. He brought a great deal of attention to the competition and his fellow Jewish athletes.

Since the Olympics, Lenny has done extensive modeling work and made numerous celebrity appearances. He has posed for *GQ, Sports Illustrated*, and *DNR Clothing* and was voted one of *People* magazine's "50 Most Beautiful People." He also competed on *Who Wants to Be a Millionaire*, where he won $32,000 for the America-Israel Friendship League.

Lenny continues to work in the water as well. He won the 100-meter backstroke at the 2002 U.S. Open and placed second in the event at the 2003 La Federation Internationalé De Natation (FINA) World Cup in Berlin, Germany. He is currently the man to beat in any backstroke competition and looks in a good position to dominate the next Olympic contest in Athens, Greece, in 2004. Lenny's career has been inspirational so far and, like his patented backstroke, shows no sign of slowing.

MORE JEWISH MALE OLYMPIANS:

Marring the 1936 Olympic Games was the last-minute decision by the U.S. Olympic Committee to remove from competition two Jewish track-and-field stars—**Marty Glickman** and **Sam Stoller.** Many people thought that the decision was made as a concession to the Nazi leader, Adolf Hitler. In 1998 the U.S. Olympic Committee issued an apology for the decision.

Henry Wittenberg, *right,* **defeating Russia's August Englas in the light heavyweight elimination match in the Olympics, Helsinki, Finland, 1952.**

Henry Wittenberg, a world-class wrestler, was undefeated for an astounding 12 years. He won gold in the 1948 Olympic Games and was named the Jewish Athlete of the Year in 1949. In 1952 Henry came out of retirement to win a silver medal at the Olympic Games in Finland. This time, he competed in the light heavyweight division. He became the first American wrestler to win two medals since 1908. Henry later served as the head coach of the U.S. Wrestling Team for the 1968 Olympic Games. He is a member of the National Wresting Hall of Fame.

At the 1984 Summer Games in Los Angeles, Jewish gymnast **Mitch Gaylord** earned four medals. He won bronze medals in the rings and parallel bars, a silver medal in the vault, and a gold medal in the team competition. He was also the first U.S. gymnast to earn a perfect 10 score in Olympic competition. Mitch was ranked the number one gymnast in America in 1983 and 1984.

PROFESSIONAL WRESTLING

GOLDBERG

Born: December 27, 1966, Tulsa, OK

I have never, nor would I ever, hide my Jewish identity.

—Goldberg on the significance of his wrestling name

Goldberg displays his charisma in the ring.

In the tradition of stereotype-breaking athletes like the power-hitting Hank Greenberg and boxing legend Benny Leonard, William "Bill" Goldberg has recently broken another barrier for Jewish competitors. Since the mid-1990s, William, known in the wrestling world simply as Goldberg, has been one of the most popular and dominating personalities in American professional wrestling. And while some may argue that wrestling is not a "real" sport, the combination of athleticism and entertainment has made it a phenomenon on a worldwide scale. Goldberg is the first big-name Jewish professional wrestler, and he has embraced this role with open arms. When he is not defeating his foes with his patented jackhammer move, Goldberg is a devout member of the Jewish community and a role model to all his young followers.

Goldberg was born December 27, 1966, and grew up in Tulsa, Oklahoma. His father is a Harvard-trained doctor and his mother is a classical musician, so it came as a bit of a surprise when Goldberg and his brothers excelled in competitive sports. Football was the young Goldberg's game. He was a commanding defensive lineman in high school and went on to play for the University of Georgia. A starter by his sophomore year, Goldberg played every game of the season and broke the school record for tackles by an interior lineman with 107. Georgia made it to the Liberty Bowl and defeated Arkansas 20–17.

In 1988 Goldberg switched to the position of nose tackle and led his team to a 9–3–0 record. At six feet four inches, 285 pounds, Goldberg was named All-Southeastern Conference by United Press International. In 1989 Goldberg made the *Football News* All-America second team. This was his best season at Georgia, and the hulking lineman made 121 tackles, breaking his own school record. He also had eight sacks. Goldberg graduated from the University of Georgia with 348 tackles, seventh in the school's history.

After college, Goldberg was drafted by the Los Angeles Rams. However, he failed to make the team in 1989 and 1990, so he decided to give the World League of American Football a try. In 1992 Goldberg led the Sacramento Surge to a WLAF Championship. Impressed with his performance, the NFL's Atlanta Falcons signed Goldberg to a contract. He played 14 games with the Falcons over three years before getting injured in a preseason game. His contract was picked up by the Carolina Panthers, but his injury kept him from making the team. Frustrated, Goldberg had to give up his NFL career in 1995, and he had no idea where to go next.

The way Goldberg tells it, a strange twist of fate brought him to wrestling. He was hanging around with some college friends and "somehow the TV wound up on professional wrestling."

Goldberg said to his friends, "Wouldn't it be a trip if that was me up there in the ring?" Goldberg says he was chided by his friends, who called him "G.I. Jew." Goldberg would have the last laugh. Soon after the incident with his friends, Goldberg met wrestler Diamond Dallas Page. The wrestling star was impressed with Goldberg's size and urged him to try a career in professional wrestling. Goldberg gave it a shot and became an instant success.

"It's a grueling job," says Goldberg of his professional wrestling career. "Let's be honest—you have to question the sanity of anybody who enters professional wrestling, not just nice little Jewish boys like me." Despite the bruises and dangerous matches, professional wrestling has been very good to Goldberg. He has become a true celebrity of the sport, with legions of loyal fans.

Apart from his towering size, Goldberg is a great performer and a witty speaker. He started in the now defunct World Championship Wrestling (WCW) and won 170 matches in his 1997 rookie season. He has since beaten such opponents as Scott Hall, Sting, Raven, and Hulk Hogan, and won the WCW World Heavyweight Championship in 1998. Since this win, Goldberg has emerged as one of the most popular wrestlers in the World Wrestling Entertainment (WWE) (the recently renamed World Wrestling Federation (WWF)) and has appeared in TV shows and movies in addition to the ring.

Goldberg has paved a new path for Jewish athletes and has added a new Jewish image to popular culture. As he says, "Nine times out of ten, people consider a nice little Jewish boy the kid who grows up and does your taxes. I've certainly broken that stereotype in many ways." Goldberg has continued the tradition of proving that Jewish athletes are just as exciting as anyone else, and he tells this constantly to his young fans. He is happy to be a role model and a symbol of Jewish athletics the world over.

SOCCER

JEFF AGOOS

Born: May 2, 1968, Geneva, Switzerland

I just put the ball in a dangerous position. That's my job.

—Jeff Agoos on playing defender

Soccer is still considered a young sport in America. It has never been as popular in the United States as it is in other countries around the world, and Major League Soccer (MLS) is still fighting for a position among the top American sports leagues. Yet a handful of talented American

Jeff Agoos, *left*, **heads a ball away from a competitor.**

players have managed to earn countrywide name recognition. Defender Jeff Agoos is one of these players. With the second most starts in U.S. team history, Jeff has established himself as one of the best American soccer players of all time. In addition to the U.S. team, Jeff has played in the Olympics, the MLS, and the highly competitive pro soccer leagues of Europe. He is one of the reasons that American soccer is growing fast in popularity.

Jeff was born on May 2, 1968, in Geneva, Switzerland. He moved to the United States in time to attend high school in Dallas and then went to college at the University of Virginia. Jeff was a fantastic college soccer player and was named freshman of the year in 1986. He was an All-American in each of his four years at Virginia and was voted Atlantic Coast Most Valuable Player in 1988. In 1989 he led the Virginia team to an NCAA championship.

While Jeff was in college, he also began training to play in the U.S. national soccer program. Before he played on the senior U.S. team, he started out on the official National Youth Teams. Then in 1988, he made his U.S. National Team debut against Guatemala. Since that game, Jeff has played in 133 international games. In 1996 Jeff tallied the game-winning assist in a U.S. World Cup qualifying game against Trinidad and Tobago. In 1997 he led the team in minutes played during World Cup qualifying games. He played in nine out of ten qualifying games, helping the United States earn a spot in the 1998 World Cup.

Although the United States lost its World Cup games, the team played much better than anyone expected. Jeff was especially impressive on defense. He helped hold Germany, a scoring powerhouse, to only two goals. The United States left the Cup with much more respect than it had received coming in. Many thought the American soccer program was finally starting to take shape. Over the next few years, Jeff Agoos would be a big part of the country's soccer growth and popularity.

During his preparation for the World Cup, Jeff was also playing in the MLS. The league started in 1995, and Jeff joined D.C. United in 1996. He was invaluable to his team in his first season, starting all 38 games, and marking one goal and five assists from his defensive position. He led United to the MLS Championship in his first season with the team. Jeff continued to play with United until after the 2000 season, when he signed with the San Jose Earthquakes. Jeff also played on the U.S. Olympic team in 2000 and helped the team to a fourth-place finish.

During the 2001 season, Jeff took one of the worst teams in the league to second place in their division and led all players in the MLS in votes for the All-Star Game with 34,711. In the playoffs, the Earthquakes shocked everyone by taking the MLS Cup. Jeff won the Defender of the Year award and was named to the AT&T MLS Best.

In 2002 the United States returned to the World Cup and made it to the quarterfinals. The team played brilliantly, defeating Portugal and Mexico. Jeff saw plenty of playing time in spite of a new wave of young defenders on the team. Soccer had finally matured in the United States, and Jeff was there to play and make it happen. Much like U.S. soccer, Jeff has only improved and become more popular as he has gotten older. He is both a classic and exciting modern player and one of the best America has to offer.

TENNIS

DICK SAVITT

Born: March 4, 1927, Orange, NJ

His contemporaries described him as almost driven, a man who hated to lose.

—*The American Jewish Historical Society on Dick Savitt*

Dick Savitt after winning Wimbledon, July 6, 1951

In the 1950s, when Dick Savitt became a world tennis champion, the idea of a great Jewish tennis player was almost unthinkable. This was not because Jewish athletes were unskilled, it was because country clubs often discriminated against Jews being members or even being allowed to use the courts. At this time, tennis was primarily a club sport. The discrimination prevented many able young prospects from getting the training that they needed to compete at the highest level. When Dick Savitt won Wimbledon in England in 1951, he shocked the sports world and proved the ability of Jews to excel in a "Gentile" game.

The road to the tennis court was not a straight path for Richard Savitt. Born in Orange, New Jersey, in 1927, Dick had an early love for the game of basketball. When his family moved to El Paso, Texas, the athletic 16-year-old joined the basketball team at El Paso High and became an All-State forward. Meanwhile, tennis was just a fun game for Dick, who entered tournaments to keep in shape for basketball.

Dick's view changed when he attended Cornell University after a brief stint in the navy. He started playing basketball for Cornell, but an unfortunate knee injury soon ruined his hopes for a starting position. Dick was heartbroken, but he realized that tennis did not aggravate his knee as much. With new determination, Dick returned to the tennis court and aimed to be the best. The sport had always come naturally to Dick, but he did not have the refinement of some of the club players. He overcame this by practicing with an unwavering discipline. Dick soon marched to the top of the Cornell tennis team, earning the number one ranking in singles.

By 1947 Dick was ranked twenty-sixth in the nation. He played tournaments constantly, striving to improve. Along the way, Dick managed to beat some big-name players on the circuit. He shot up in the rankings, taking the seventeenth spot by 1949. In 1950 Dick's tennis game took off. He won the Eastern Intercollegiate Tournament, the East Clay Court Tournament, and the New York State Tournament. He then proceeded to the 1950 Nationals and made it all the way to the semifinals before losing to Art Larsen. Dick had hoped to make the finals at Nationals, but his game had improved so much he couldn't help but be pleased. He had come a long way since the days of smacking tennis balls around for fun.

After the Nationals, Dick traveled to Australia to play in his first Grand Slam (major tennis) event, the Australian Open. He was nervous to play in front of the large crowds but managed to relax enough to beat tough competitor John Bromwich early in the tournament. His next match was a bit harder. Dick was up against Australian star Frank Sedgeman. Sedgeman took an early lead in the match with a powerful serve and strategically placed shots. But Dick embarked on a comeback midway through the match. "I started hitting winners all over the place," said Savitt. After defeating Sedgemen, Dick had no trouble winning the finals. He defeated Ken McGregor 6–3, 2–6, 6–3, 6–1.

After conquering the Australian Open, Dick decided to give Wimbledon, the oldest Grand Slam event, a shot. He felt confident about his game, but his journey to the finals was not easy. Dick struggled early in the tournament with the Danish player Kurt Nielson. Even though Dick was the better player, he couldn't get a handle on his ground strokes and took a long five sets to defeat Nielson 6–4, 1–6, 6–3, 8–10, 6–4. His next match was easier. He beat his opponent in straight sets. Dick managed to settle into his game after the win and upset America's top-seeded player, Art Larsen, 6–1, 6–4, 6–4. He blasted the baseline throughout the match with perfectly placed backhands. After his win over Larsen, Dick was in the semifinals against America's number two player, Herbert Flam. Dick was ranked sixth at the time, and both players were coming off of big upset wins.

The first two sets belonged to Flam. He used a soft-hitting, strategic style of play and gave Dick nothing to hit. Dick Savitt was known for his power in the tennis world, and it upset his game to get into a battle of light strokes. Flam won eleven of the first thirteen games before Dick began his comeback. Dick started to match Flam's game, and he slowly took over the pace of the match. Once he felt he was in control, Dick upped the pace. He began to take risks and rush toward the net. Eventually, he overpowered Flam and beat him in five sets.

The next day, hot off his win, Dick beat Ken McGregor in straight sets. It was as if he had already decided to win the match. After his hard-fought semifinal win, the match with McGregor seemed easy. Just like that, Dick Savitt, the boy who had never taken formal tennis lessons, was the Wimbledon champion. After only a few years of serious competitive play, Dick had reached the pinnacle of his career.

Dick prepared for the next Grand Slam event, the U.S. Open. But he lost the chance to win his third Grand Slam because of a leg infection. After this disappointment, Savitt's coach inexplicably kept him out of the Davis Cup. Dick was so distraught about the injustice that he retired at the age of 25, returning to the game only on a part-time basis.

Despite the quick ups and downs of his career, Dick Savitt remains the only Jewish player to win a Wimbledon singles title. He was a hero to the next generation of Jewish players and proved that a tennis champion didn't need a fancy country club membership to compete. After Dick's big wins in 1951, more young Jewish athletes began to pick up a racquet and dream of the grass courts of Wimbledon. Dick is a member of the International Jewish Sports Hall of Fame and was inducted into the International Tennis Hall of Fame in 1976.

JULIE HELDMAN

Born: December 8, 1945, Berkeley, CA

She was a player that sort of slices and dices and drives you crazy. She was very smart and used all her capability on the court.

—*Tennis great Martina Navratilova on Julie Heldman*

Julie Heldman serves to Margaret Court in a singles match, 1975.

For most of her life, Julie Heldman has lived and breathed the game of tennis. In the 1960s, she was a top professional on the circuit and a medal-winning Olympian for the United States. In the 1970s, she became a tennis commentator, broadcasting for NBC, CBS, and PBS. Julie has been described as "quick," "vivacious," and "one of the toughest competitors the game has known." In her prime, she started successful all-women tennis tours and broke new ground in female sportscasting. Julie has worked tirelessly to bring the money and interest in women's tennis to equal footing with the men's game.

Julie was born December 8, 1945, into a family obsessed with tennis. Her father, Julius, was the 1936 U.S. Junior Champion, and her mother, Gladys, was the publisher of *World Tennis* magazine. Julie began hitting the courts when she was eight, and by age 12 had earned her first national title. At the 1958 Canadian Junior Championships, Julie became the first 12-year-old to win. She followed up her early victory with titles in the 1960 and 1963 U.S. Junior Championships.

As she graduated to the adult professional ranks, Julie soon became one of the best players in the United States. In 1963 she was ranked number 10 in the country, and by 1964 she had worked her way up to number seven. Julie was playing for Stanford University in 1964, and she made both the collegiate doubles and singles finals that year. Her aggressive play and killer instinct earned her a spot on the 1968 Olympic team in Mexico City, where she won gold, silver, and bronze medals. The gold and silver were in doubles, and the bronze was in the singles competition.

The following year, Julie reached the number five national ranking. Then she won the Italian Open and rocketed up to number two in the United States. Julie was playing the best tennis of her career and surprised many when she left the United States Tennis Association (USTA) to play on the

Virginia Slims circuit in Houston. Supported by Julie's mom, this contest was the first all-women's tour in professional tennis. It became a roaring success and eventually merged with the USTA to become the modern Women's Tennis Association (WTA). The popularity of the women's tour also helped raise the salaries of female tennis professionals.

In the early 1970s, Julie made the semifinals at the French, Australian, and U.S. Opens but never managed to make it to the finals. She retired from professional tennis soon after the 1974 U.S. Open and started a second career doing telecasts on major television stations.

By 1976 Julie became the first woman to broadcast men's tennis. In the late 1970s, Julie worked for numerous high-profile stations, using her vibrant personality to make the commentary exciting and informative.

After broadcasting, Julie attended law school at the University of California, Los Angeles. She was named the school's Law Graduate of the Year in 1981. Julie was inducted into the International Jewish Sports Hall of Fame in 2000. She is remembered not only as a great tennis player and TV personality but as a pioneer for the game of women's tennis. The triumph of the all-women tour combined with her beliefs about gender equality helped make the tennis world a welcome place for talented female players.

MORE JEWISH TENNIS STARS:

Harold Solomon was ranked number five in the world in 1980 and was often called the "human backboard" because of his ability to return any shot. He began playing tennis at the age of five and rose to number 15 in the world after an All-American tennis career at Rice University. From 1974 to 1981, Harold made the top 25 rankings every year and won

21 different singles titles. Although he made the finals at the French Open and the semifinals at the U.S. Open, Harold never won a Grand Slam tournament. He is remembered for his gritty, lob-heavy style of play.

Elise Burgin made a name for herself as one of the best doubles players in the 1980s. She played with stars like Martina Navratilova and Pam Shriver. Like Julie Heldman, Elise was a key player at Stanford University, where she was an All-American from 1981 to 1984. In her last year at Stanford, she won the NCAA doubles championship with teammate Linda Gates. Elise played in all four Grand Slam events and reached the fourth round of the U.S. Open in 1982. After retiring from tennis, Elise became a successful television commentator.

Brad Gilbert was another great player in the 1980s and 1990s. With a style that the *New York Times* called "winning ugly," Gilbert managed to beat top players such as John McEnroe, Boris Becker, and Michael Chang. Brad relished his ability to win without using power. He played great strategic tennis and stayed in the top 25 for most of his career. After he retired, he coached Andre Agassi to six Grand Slam victories. Agassi once said, "Brad is clearly the greatest coach of all time."

Nicknamed Marathon Man, **Aaron Krickstein** went pro when he was only 16 years old and became the youngest player to win a tour singles title. His nickname came from his ability to come from behind. Aaron never gave up a match and rallied back to beat tough opponents. He was ranked number eight in 1989 and won four titles in the 1990s.

MACCABEE AWARD
Jewish Athlete of the Year

1974	Ernie Grunfeld, Basketball
	Larry Horowitz, Basketball
1975	Esther Roth, Track & Field
1976	Esther Roth, Track & Field
	Irene Szewinska, Track & Field
1977	Dan Gardner, Track & Field
1978	Mike Rossman, Boxer
1979	Nancy Lieberman, Basketball
1980	Amy Alcott, Golf
	Steve Stone, Baseball
1981	Sharon Shapiro, Gymnastics
1982	Marty Hogan, Racquetball
1983	Mitch Gaylord, Gymnastics
1984	Mitch Gaylord, Gymnastics
1985	Mark Roth, Bowling
1987	John E. Frank, Football
1988	Doug Heir, Wheelchair Athletics
1989	Harris Barton, Football
1990	Judy Blumberg, Ice Dancing
1991	Judy Blumberg, Ice Dancing
1992	Yael Arad, Judo
1993	Gilad Jankowitz, Fitness
1994	Shawn Green, Baseball
1995	Doug Heir, Wheelchair Athletics
1996	Doug Heir, Wheelchair Athletics
1997	Shawn Green, Baseball
1998	Shawn Green, Baseball
1999	Lenny Krayzelburg, Swimming
2000	Lenny Krayzelburg, Swimming
2001	Dr. Ziv Bar-Shira, Wheelchair Sports
	Alex Averbuch, Track & Field
2002	Gal Friedman, Windsurfing
	Zhanna Pintussevich-Block, Track & Field

STATISTICS

JEFF AGOOS

Year	Team	Regular season				Playoffs			
		GP/GS	G	A	P	GP/GS	G	A	P
1996	D.C. United	32/32	1	5	7	6/6	0	0	0
1997	D.C. United	29/27	1	3	5	5/5	0	0	0
1998	D.C. United	21/20	1	4	6	6/6	1	3	5
1999	D.C. United	30/29	2	2	6	6/6	0	1	1
2000	D.C. United	23/23	1	3	5	—	—	—	—
2001	San Jose Earthquakes	20/20	2	2	6	6/6	0	1	1
2002	San Jose Earthquakes	12/9	0	0	0	2/2	0	0	0
	Totals	167/160	8	19	35	31/31	1	5	7

GP=Games Played, GS=Games Started, G=Goals, A=Assists, P=Points

Also played professionally with Maryland Bays (A-League) in 1991, Dallas Sidekicks (MISL) in 1992, and SV Wehen (German Third Division) in 1995 — statistics not available. CAPS (international games played)=133

Career Highlights:

1986 Named Soccer America co-freshman of the year
1989 Member of University of Virginia NCAA co-championship; named to second All-American squad
1992 Silver medal with futsal team in Hong Kong
1996 Won U.S. Open Cup with D.C. United
1996, 1997, 1998 MLS Cup titles with D.C. United
1997, 1999 Named to MLS Best XI
1998 International debut on January 13 vs. Guatemala; scored first international goal three days later, also against Guatemala; won Interamerican Cup Championship with D.C. United; World Cup
1999 Bronze medal FIFA Confederation's Cup in Mexico
2000 Played every minute at Olympics in Sydney, 4th place finish.
2001 Captained San Jose Earthquakes to first MLS Cup victory; named MLS Defender of the Year
2002 Started all three first round games for the United States in 2002 World Cup, scored winning goal vs. Portugal; named to Gold Cup Best XI; scored winning goal in Gold Cup vs. Costa Rica

SASHA COHEN

Career Highlights:

1997 Junior Olympics, Intermediate, 5th

1998 Pacific Coast Sectionals, 2nd; U.S. National Championships, 6th; SW Pacific Regionals, 2nd

1999 Pacific Coast Sectionals, 1st; SW Pacific Regionals, 1st ; Gardena Winter Trophy, 1st; JGP Sweden, 1st; U.S. Junior National Championships, silver

2000 Pacific Coast Sectionals, 1st; U.S. National Championships, silver; World Junior Championships, 6th

2001 Trophee Lalique (Grand Prix), 3rd; Finaldia Trophy, 1st

2002 U.S. National Championships, silver ; World Championships, 4th; Winter Olympics, 4th; Skate Canada (Grand Prix), 1st; Trophee Lalique, 1st; Cup of Russia, 2nd; Sears Figure Skating Open, 1st; Crest Whitestrips International Figure Skating Challenge, 1st

2003 U.S. National Championships, bronze; ABC International Figure Skating Challenge, 3rd; World Championships, 4th; Grand Prix Final, 1st

2003 Received the "Women of Achievement in Sports" Award from St. Francis Hospital and Medical Center

JAY FIEDLER

Year	Team	G	QB	A	C	YD	%	PTD	I	R	RTD	S	F
1998	Minnesota	5	22.6	7	3	41	42.9	0	1	4	0	0	0
1999	Jacksonville	8	83.5	94	61	656	64.9	2	2	13	0	7	1
2000	Miami	15	74.5	357	204	2402	57.1	14	14	54	1	23	2
2001	Miami	16	80.3	450	273	3290	60.7	20	19	73	4	27	6
2002	Miami	11	85.2	292	179	2024	61.3	14	9	28	3	13	3
2003	Miami	12	72.4	314	179	2138	57.0	11	13	34	3	19	7
	Totals	67	78.1	1514	899	10551	59.4	61	58	206	11	89	73

G=Games, QB=Quarterback rating, A=Attempts, C=Completions, YD=Yards, %=Percentage, PTD=Passing Touchdowns, I=Interceptions, R=Rushes, RTD=Rushing Touchdown, S=Sacks, F=Fumbles

Career Highlights:

1991–1993 Starter at Dartmouth

First Jewish starting quarterback in NFL since the 1960s

GOLDBERG

Career Highlights:

1989 Drafted by the Los Angeles Rams
1992 Won World League of American Football Championship with Sacramento Surge
1992–1994 Played 14 games with the Atlanta Falcons (NFL)
1995 Signed by the Carolina Panthers but retired because of injury
1998 WCW World Heavyweight Champion; named PWI Rookie of the Year
1998, 1999 WCW U.S. Champion
1999 WCW Tag Team Champion (with Bret Hart)
2003 WWE World Heavyweight Title

SHAWN GREEN

Season	Team	G	AB	R	H	2B	3B	HR	RBI	BB	SB	AVG	A	E
1993	Toronto	3	6	0	0	0	0	0	0	0	0	.000	0	0
1994	Toronto	14	33	1	3	1	0	0	1	1	1	.091	2	0
1995	Toronto	121	379	52	109	31	4	15	54	20	1	.288	9	6
1996	Toronto	132	422	52	118	32	3	11	45	33	5	.280	10	2
1997	Toronto	135	429	57	123	22	4	16	53	36	14	.287	6	3
1998	Toronto	158	630	106	175	33	4	35	100	50	35	.278	14	7
1999	Toronto	153	614	134	190	45	0	42	123	66	20	.309	5	1
2000	LA	162	610	98	164	44	4	24	99	90	24	.269	9	6
2001	LA	161	619	121	184	31	4	49	125	72	20	.297	8	6
2002	LA	158	582	110	166	31	1	42	114	93	8	.285	7	2
2003	LA	160	611	84	171	49	2	19	85	68	6	.280	9	5
	Totals	1357	4935	815	1403	319	26	253	799	529	134	.284	79	38

G=Games, AB=At Bats, R=Runs, H=Hits, 2B=Doubles, 3B=Triples, HR=Home runs, RBI=Runs Batted In, BB=Bases on Balls (Walks), SB=Stolen Bases, AVG=Batting Average, A=Assists, E=Errors

"HAMMERIN'" HANK GREENBERG

Season	Team	G	AB	R	H	2B	3B	HR	RBI	BB	SB	AVG	A	E
1930	Detroit	1	1	0	0	0	0	0	0	0	0	.000	0	0
1933	Detroit	117	449	59	135	33	3	12	87	46	6	.301	84	14
1934	Detroit	153	593	118	201	63	7	26	139	63	9	.339	99	16
1935	Detroit	152	619	121	203	46	16	36	170	87	4	.328	9	13
1936	Detroit	12	46	10	16	6	2	1	16	9	1	.348	9	1
1937	Detroit	154	594	137	200	49	14	40	183	102	8	.337	102	13
1938	Detroit	155	559	144	175	23	4	58	146	119	7	.315	120	14
1939	Detroit	138	500	112	156	42	7	33	112	91	8	.312	75	9
1940	Detroit	148	573	129	195	50	8	41	150	93	6	.340	14	15
1941	Detroit	19	67	12	18	5	1	2	12	16	1	.269	0	3
1945	Detroit	78	270	47	84	20	2	13	60	42	3	.311	3	0
1946	Detroit	142	523	91	145	29	5	44	127	80	5	.277	93	15
1947	Pittsburgh	125	402	71	100	13	2	25	74	104	0	.249	79	9
	Totals	1394	5193	1051	1628	379	71	331	1276	852	58	.313	741	122

G=Games, AB=At Bats, R=Runs, H=Hits, 2B=Doubles, 3B=Triples, HR=Home runs, RBI=Runs Batted In, BB=Bases on Balls (Walks), SB=Stolen Bases, AVG=Batting Average, A=Assists, E=Errors

Career Highlights:

1935, 1940 American League (AL) Most Valuable Player
1935, 1937, 1940, 1946 led league in RBIs
1935, 1938, 1940, 1946 AL Home Run Champion; led league in home runs
1937–1940 All-Star
1948 First Jewish owner-general manager in baseball (Cleveland Indians)
1956 First Jewish major leaguer elected to Baseball Hall of Fame
1958 Became part owner of Chicago White Sox

JEFF HALPERN

Year	Team	GP	Goals	Assists	Points (regular)	Points (playoffs)
1999–00	Washington	79	18	11	29	0
2000–01	Washington	80	21	21	42	0
2001–02	Washington	48	5	14	19	0
2002–03	Washington	82	13	21	34	1
	Totals	289	57	67	124	1

GP=Games Played

Career Highlights:
1995–1999 Scored 60 goals and 82 assists in 131 games at Princeton
1997–1998, 1998–1999 Earned spot on ECAC All-Star Team

JULIE HELDMAN

Matches Won: 57   Matches Lost: 30
Grand Slams: 47 won, 21 lost

Career Highlights:

1958 Captured first title (Canadian Junior Championships) and became first 12-year-old to win a national crown
1960, 1963 Won U.S. Junior Title
1963 Ranked number 10 in United States
1964 Ranked number 7 in United States
1966, 1969 Member of USA Federation Cup team
1968 Won gold, silver, and bronze at Olympics
1968–1969 Ranked number 2 in United States
1969 Reached quarterfinals at Wimbledon; won Italian Open Title; won three gold medals at Maccabiah Games
1969, 1974 Ranked number 5 in world
1970 Left USTA to play in Virginia Slims Circuit Tournament in Houston; reached semifinals of French Open; ranked number 9 in world
1974 Reached semifinals of Australian Open; reached semifinals of U.S. Open
2000 Inducted into International Jewish Sports Hall of Fame

ART HEYMAN

Season	Team	G	R	A	P	PPG	FG%	FT%
1963–64	New York	75	298	256	1153	15.4	.431	.685
1964–65	New York	55	99	79	316	5.7	.427	.667
1965–66	Cincinnati	17	17	11	50	2.9	.346	.636
1967–68	Pittsburgh	73	496	276	1349	18.5	.432	.731
1968–69	Minnesota	71	494	217	1022	14.4	.421	.697
1969–70	Miami	19	57	20	140	7.4	.443	.708
	Totals	310	1461	859	4030	13.0	.427	.703

G=Games, R=Rebounds, A=Assists, P=Points, PPG=Average points per game, FG%=Percentage of field goals made to field goals attempted, FT%=percentage of free throws made to free throws attempted

Career Highlights:

1961–1963 All-American at Duke University
1963 Voted college basketball player of the year by Associated Press and *Sporting News*; number 1; overall draft pick (New York Knicks); First Team All-NBA team
1974 Inducted into Helms Hall of Fame
1993 Inducted into Jewish Sports Hall of Fame

SANDY KOUFAX

Year	Team	W	L	ERA	G	I	H	SO	BB
1955	Dodgers	2	2	3.02	12	41.2	33	30	28
1956	Dodgers	2	4	4.91	16	58.2	66	30	29
1957	Dodgers	5	4	3.88	34	104.1	83	122	51
1958	Dodgers	11	11	4.48	40	158.2	132	131	105
1959	Dodgers	8	6	4.05	35	153.1	136	173	92
1960	Dodgers	8	13	3.91	37	175.0	133	197	100
1961	Dodgers	18	13	3.52	42	255.2	212	269	96
1962	Dodgers	14	7	2.54	28	184.1	134	216	57
1963	Dodgers	25	5	1.88	40	311.0	214	306	58
1964	Dodgers	19	5	1.74	29	223.0	154	223	53
1965	Dodgers	26	8	2.04	43	335.2	216	382	71
1966	Dodgers	27	9	1.73	41	323.0	241	317	77
	Totals	165	87	2.76	397	2324.1	1754	2396	817

W=Wins, L=Losses, ERA=Earned Run Average, G=Games, I=Innings, H=Hits,
SO=Strikeouts, BB=Bases on Balls (walks)

Career Highlights:

1961 Established National League strikeout record of 269
1962–1966 Won ERA Title
1963 National League MVP
1963, 1965 World Series MVP
1963, 1965 Hickok Belt Pro Athlete of the Year Award
1963, 1965, 1966 Cy Young Award
1965 First in MLB to pitch four no-hitters; pitched perfect game vs. Chicago; record 382
   strikeouts; Babe Ruth award for outstanding performance in World Series
1972 Elected to Baseball Hall of Fame
1999 Named to All-Century Team

LENNY KRAYZELBURG

Year	Location	Event	Time	O, W, A
1999	Sydney	50m back	24.99	W, A
1999	Sydney	100m back	53.60	W, A
1999	Sydney	200m back	1:55.87	W, A
2000	Sydney	100m back	53.72	O
2000	Sydney	200m back	1:56.76	O
2000	Sydney	400m MR	3:33.73	O, W, A

O=Olympic record, W=World record, A=American record

Medals:

1997 Pan Pacific Championships: first place in 100m back, 200m back, 400m medley relay (MR)

1998 Goodwill Games: gold for 200m back, silver for 100m back; World Championships: gold for 100m back and 200m back, silver 400m MR

1999 Pan Pacific Championships: first place in 100m back, 200m back, 400m MR

2000 Short Course World Championships: first for 400m MR; Olympic Games: gold for 100m back, 200m back, and 400m MR

Career Highlights:

1997–1999 Phillips Performance Award

1997–2000 All-Star team member

1998 USOC SportsMan of the Year finalist

1999, 2000 USA Swimming Swimmer of the Year

2000 Featured in *People* magazine's "50 Most Beautiful People" as an "Olympic Beauty"

BENNY LEONARD

Fights	Wins	Losses	Wins by KO	Wins by Decision	No Decision	Technical KO	Draws
212	85	5	69	1	121	—	1

KO=Knockout

Career Highlights:

1917–1925 World lightweight boxing champion, longest reign in history of Lightweight Division, retired undefeated

1955 Inducted into *Ring* magazine's Boxing Hall of Fame

1980 Inducted into World Boxing Hall of Fame

1990 Inducted into International Boxing Hall of Fame

SID LUCKMAN

Year	Team	G	A	C	YD	%	PTD	I	R	RYD	RTD
1939	Chicago	11	51	23	636	45.1	5	4	24	42	0
1940	Chicago	11	105	48	941	45.7	4	9	23	-65	0
1941	Chicago	11	119	68	1181	57.1	9	6	18	18	1
1942	Chicago	11	105	57	1023	54.3	10	13	13	-6	0
1943	Chicago	10	202	110	2194	54.5	28	12	22	-40	1
1944	Chicago	7	143	71	1018	49.7	11	12	20	-96	1
1945	Chicago	10	217	117	1725	53.9	14	10	36	-118	0
1946	Chicago	11	229	110	1826	48.0	17	16	25	-76	0
1947	Chicago	12	323	176	2712	54.5	24	31	10	86	1
1948	Chicago	12	163	89	1047	54.6	13	14	8	11	0
1949	Chicago	11	50	22	200	44.0	1	3	3	4	0
1950	Chicago	11	37	13	180	35.1	1	2	2	1	0
	Totals	128	1744	904	14686	51.8	137	132	204	-239	4

G=Games, A=Attempts, C=Completions, YD=Yards, %=Percentage, PTD=Passing Touchdowns, I=Interceptions, R=Rushes, RYD=Rushing Yards, RTD=Rushing Touchdowns

Career Highlights:

1940, 1941, 1943, 1946 Led Chicago Bears to win NFL Championship
1941–1944 All-Pro
1941–1944, 1947 All-NFL
1943 First to pass 400 yards in one game (November 14, 433 yards vs. New York); won Joe Carr Trophy for MVP in NFL
1960 Inducted into College Football Hall of Fame
1965 Elected to Pro Football Hall of Fame

RON MIX

Total Games Played: 142
1960 Los Angeles Chargers
1961–1969 San Diego Chargers
1971 Oakland Raiders

Career Highlights:

1961–1968 Pro Bowl
1962 Chargers MVP
1969 Named to All-Time AFL Team by Pro Football Hall of Fame
1978 Inducted into Chargers Hall of Fame
1979 Inducted into Pro Football Hall of Fame (sixth lineman ever inducted)
1980 Inducted into International Jewish Sports Hall of Fame
2000 Named to Chargers All-Time Team

"SLAPSIE" MAXIE ROSENBLOOM

Fights	Wins	Losses	Wins by KO	Wins by Decision	No Decision	Technical KO	Draws	No Contest
299	210	38	19	—	23	3	26	2

KO=Knockout

Career Highlights:

1930–1934 World light heavyweight champion
1972 Elected to *Ring* magazine's Boxing Hall of Fame
1993 Elected into International Boxing Hall of Fame

BARNEY ROSS

Fights	Wins	Losses	Wins by KO	Wins by Decision	No Decision	Technical KO	Draws
81	72	4	22	—	2	8	3

KO=Knockout

Career Highlights:

1933–1935 World lightweight champion; World junior welterweight champion
1934, 1935–1938 World welterweight champion
1934, 1935 *Ring* magazine's Fighter of the Year
1956 Elected to Boxing Hall of Fame
1981 Inducted into World Boxing Hall of Fame
1990 Inducted into International Boxing Hall of Fame

DICK SAVITT

Career Highlights:

1951 Won Wimbeldon Singles Championship, Australian Singles Crown, named number 1 player to U.S. Davis Cup Team, ranked number 3 in world
1952, 1958, 1961 Won U.S. National Indoor Singles Championship (first person to win this crown 3 times)
1956 Ranked number 1 in United States
1961 Won both singles and doubles (with Mike Franks) at Maccabiah Games, Israel
1976 Elected to International Tennis Hall of Fame

DOLPH SCHAYES

Season	Team	G	R	A	P	PPG	FG%	FT%
1948–49	Syracuse	63	0	0	809	12.8	0	.722
1949–50	Syracuse	64	0	259	1072	16.8	.385	.774
1950–51	Syracuse	66	1080	251	1121	17.0	.357	.752
1951–52	Syracuse	63	773	182	868	13.8	.355	.807
1952–53	Syracuse	71	920	227	1262	17.8	.374	.827
1953–54	Syracuse	72	870	214	1228	17.1	.380	.827
1954–55	Syracuse	72	887	213	1333	18.5	.383	.833
1955–56	Syracuse	72	891	200	1472	20.4	.387	.858
1956–57	Syracuse	72	1008	229	1617	22.5	.379	.904
1957–58	Syracuse	72	1022	224	1791	24.9	.398	.904
1958–59	Syracuse	72	962	178	1534	21.3	.387	.864
1959–60	Syracuse	75	959	256	1689	22.5	.401	.893
1960–61	Syracuse	79	960	296	1868	23.6	.372	.868
1961–62	Syracuse	56	439	120	822	14.7	.357	.897
1962–63	Syracuse	66	375	175	627	9.5	.388	.879
1963–64	Philadelphia	24	110	48	134	5.6	.308	.807
	Totals	1059	11256	3072	19247	18.2	.380	.849

G=Games, R=Rebounds, A=Assists, P=Points, PPG=Average points per game,
FG%=Percentage of field goals made to field goals attempted, FT%=percentage of free
throws made to free throws attempted

Career Highlights:

1948 NYU All-American
1949 NBL Rookie of the Year
1951–1962 NBA All-Star
1952–55, 1957–58 All-NBA First Team
1955 NBA Championship
1970 NBA 25th Anniversary team
1972 Elected to Naismith Memorial Basketball Hall of Fame
1996 Named one of the 50 Greatest Players in NBA

MARK SPITZ

Records:

1967 400m freestyle 4:10.06

1972 Olympics: 100m butterfly 54.27, 200m free 1:52.78, 200m butterfly 2:00.07, 400m free relay, first in world to win seven Olympic gold medals

Overall during career, set 32 world records: 25 individual, 7 relay

Medals:

1967 Pan American Games: gold for 100m fly, 200m fly, 400m free relay, 800m free relay, 400m MR

1968 Olympics: gold for 400m free relay, 800m free relay; silver for 100m fly; bronze for 100m free

1972 Olympics: gold for 100m free, 200m free, 100m fly, 200m fly, 400m free relay, 800m free relay, 400m MR

Career Highlights:

1966–1972 NCAA 8–1st place, 1–2nd, 2–3rd; AAU 24–1st, 6–2nd, 1–3rd

1967, 1971, 1972 Named World Swimmer of the Year by *Swimming World*

1971 AAU James E. Sullivan Award

1972 AAU Swimming Award; named World Athlete of the Year; Associated Press Male Athlete of the Year

1977 Inducted into International Swimming Hall of Fame as Honor Swimmer

KERRI STRUG

Career Highlights:

1990 American Classic: 1st all-around, vault, uneven bars, floor exercise

1991–1997 Member of Senior National Team

1992 Olympics: bronze for team, 14th all-around, youngest member at Games; U.S. Olympic Trials: 3rd all-around

1993 Coca-Cola National Championships: bronze for uneven bars; U.S. Olympic Festival: 1st uneven bars, 2nd all-around, balance beam, floor exercise; Hilton Challenge: 1st team, 7th all-around; World Championship: 5th all-around, 6th floor exercise

1994 Team World Championships: silver for team

1995 Coca-Cola National Championships: bronze for uneven bars; U.S. Olympic Festival: gold for all-around, uneven bars, bronze for balance beam; World Championships: bronze for team

1996 Olympics: gold for team; Coca-Cola National Championships: silver for vault and floor exercise; McDonald's American Cup: 1st all-around, balance beam, floor exercise, 2nd vault, uneven bars; U.S. Olympic Trials: 2nd all-around; McDonald's International Gymnastics Championships: 4th; Featured on "Ten Most Interesting People," *Barbara Walters Special*; member of World Gymnastics Tour and MGM/Ice Capades

JAMILA WIDEMAN

Season	Team	G	R	A	P	PPG	FG%	FT%
1997	Los Angeles	28	57	103	84	3.0	.236	.794
1998	Los Angeles	25	22	57	48	1.9	.279	.724
1999	Cleveland	26	34	51	56	2.2	.273	.647
2000	Portland	5	4	2	0	0.0	.000	.000
	Totals	84	116	213	188	2.2	.254	.738

G=Games, R=Rebounds, A=Assists, P=Points, PPG=Average points per game,
FG%=Percentage of field goals made to field goals attempted, FT%=percentage of free
throws made to free throws attempted

Career Highlights:

1992–1993 *Parade* First Team High School (H.S.) All-American; *USA Today* First Team H.S.
All-American; *USA Today* Top 25; Converse H.S. All-American; Kodak H.S. All-American;
Street and Smith's Second Team H.S. Preseason All-American; Gatorade Regional (New
England) H.S. Player of the Year; Gatorade (Massachusetts) H.S. Player of the Year

1993–1994 U.S. Olympic Festival (West Squad Alternate); Pac-10 All-Freshman; Stanford
Coaches Award

1995–1997 Led Stanford to NCAA Final Four

1997 Voted MVP of NCAA West Regional Tournament; ranked number 8 in WNBA

1998 Ranked number 10 in WNBA

1999 *USA Today Weekend*'s Most Caring Athlete Award; played for Elitzur Ramla in the
Israeli Basketball League

FURTHER READING AND WEBSITES

Horvitz, Peter S., and Joachim Horvitz. *The Big Book of Jewish Athletes: Biographies and
Anecdotes of Great Jews in Sports.* New York: SPI Books, 2003.

Horvitz, Peter S. and Joachim Horvitz. *The Big Book of Jewish Baseball.* New York: SPI
Books, 2001.

Levine, Peter. *Ellis Island to Ebbets Field: Sport and the American Jewish Experience.* United
Kingdom: Oxford University Press, 1992.

Slater, Robert. *Great Jews in Sports.* New York: Jonathan David Publishers, 2000.

JewishSports.com at <http://www.jewishsports.com/jewsinsports.htm>

Jewish Sports Hall of Fame at <http://jewishsportshalloffame.com>

Jewish Virtual Library at <http://www.us-israel.org/index.html>

Jews in Sports Online at <http://www.jewsinsports.org/>

INDEX

PHOTO ACKNOWLEDGMENTS

Images in this book are used with the permission of: © Bettmann/CORBIS, p. 4; © Underwood & Underwood/CORBIS, pp. 6, 27; © Bettmann/CORBIS, pp. 10, 21, 29, 33, 39, 41, 45, 62, 69, 79; © AFP/CORBIS, p. 13; © Reuters NewMedia Inc./CORBIS, p. 17; © Philadelphia 76ers, p. 18; © Getty Images, Getty Images North America, p. 23; © John Springer Collection/CORBIS, p. 36; © SportsChrome East/West, John Williamson, p. 48; © SportsChrome East/West, Rob Tringali, pp. 52, 55, 58; © Getty Images, Getty Images AsiaPac, p. 66; © Duomo/CORBIS, p. 70; © SportsChrome East/West, Bongarts, p. 73; © Hulton|Archive by Getty Images, p. 76.

Front cover: © SportsChrome East/West, Michael Zito; © SportsChrome East/West, Rob Tringali; © Bettmann/CORBIS; © Miami Dolphins